DON'T REST ON YOUR LAURELS

DR. DHAVAL MAHETA
PROFESSOR

"None can destroy iron, but its own rust can. Likewise, none can destroy a person but his own mindset can"

— Ratan Tata, Indian Industrialist and Philanthropist

References
Appendix: Self Assessment Questionnaire

THE ESSENCE OF DON'T REST ON YOUR LAUREALS

In a peaceful forest, the Rabbit and the Tortoise decided to race. The Rabbit, being much faster, quickly left the Tortoise behind. Confident he would win, the Rabbit decided to take a nap. He thought he had plenty of time.

The Tortoise, however, kept moving slowly but steadily. He passed the sleeping Rabbit and kept going. When the Rabbit woke up and raced to the finish line, he found that the Tortoise had already won the race.

The Rabbit's mistake was thinking he could relax and still win. He had ***rested on his laurel's***, assuming success was guaranteed. Meanwhile, the Tortoise's steady effort paid off because he didn't stop or get complacent.

This story teaches us that to avoid the pitfalls of resting on our laurels, we must stay focused and keep working hard, no matter how successful we've been. The key to ongoing success is to never become too comfortable or stop pushing forward. This book will guide you on how to stay motivated, adapt to changes, and continuously improve. By embracing these principles, you can ensure that you remain ahead and continue to succeed, no matter how far you've come.

WHY THIS BOOK MATTERS

In a world that is constantly evolving, resting on past achievements can be a major barrier to continued success and personal growth. *"Don't Rest on Your Laurels"* book is essential for everyone because it addresses a universal challenge of how to maintain momentum and strive for improvement, no matter how successful you have been.

1. Overcoming Complacency: The book provides practical strategies to help readers avoid the pitfalls of complacency. Many individuals and organizations find that initial success can lead to a false sense of security. This book teaches how to stay motivated and keep pushing forward, ensuring that past achievements don't become a ceiling on future potential. This is the reason that book title is *"Don't Rest on your Laurels"*.

2. Continuous Learning and Innovation: As the world changes rapidly, staying relevant requires ongoing learning and adaptability. This book emphasizes the importance of lifelong learning and innovation, offering actionable advice on how to integrate these practices into daily life.

3. Setting and Achieving New Goals: Success often leads to a plateau where setting new, meaningful goals can be challenging. *"Don't Rest on Your Laurels"* guides readers through the process of setting and achieving new objectives, helping them maintain ambition and drive.

4. Balancing Success with Well-being: Achieving success can come with its own set of challenges, including burnout and stress. The book provides insights into maintaining a healthy work-life balance, ensuring that the pursuit of excellence does not compromise personal well-being.

5. Inspiring Leadership and Legacy: For those in leadership positions, the book offers strategies for leading by example and building a lasting legacy. It highlights the role of mentorship and the impact of inspiring others to achieve their best.

In today's fast-paced world, the stakes are higher than ever. Technological advancements, global competition, and rapidly changing markets mean that the landscape is constantly shifting. What worked yesterday might not work tomorrow. The only way to stay ahead is to keep moving forward—to never be satisfied with the status quo, no matter how successful it may seem. It offers a roadmap for turning past successes into a foundation for future achievements, making it a valuable resource for individuals and leaders alike.

This book is not just for business leaders or entrepreneurs; it's for anyone who has achieved something significant and wants to maintain and build on that success. Whether you're a student who has just graduated with top honors, a professional at the peak of your career, or someone who has reached a personal milestone, the lessons in this book apply to you.

Chapter 1: Concept of Don't Rest on Your Laurels

1.1. The Subtle Shift

Success is a wonderful feeling. After working hard to achieve something, it's easy to relax and enjoy the rewards. However, there's a hidden risk becoming too comfortable with past accomplishments. This subtle shift from ambition to complacency often happens without realizing it. One minute you're pushing yourself, and the next, you're ***resting on your laurels***, relying on old successes rather than striving for new ones. Redundancy and complacency are interconnected, as redundancy often creates a sense of comfort that can lead to stagnation. When individuals repeatedly follow the same routines or rely on past successes, they may become overconfident and stop seeking growth or improvement. This habitual repetition fosters a mindset where one assumes that what has worked before will always work in the future, leading to a diminished focus on innovation and adaptation. For instance, an athlete who consistently wins competitions might rely solely on their existing training regimen, believing it is sufficient. Over time, this lack of new strategies or effort to improve can result in declining performance, as they fail to account for changes in competition or their own abilities. This demonstrates how redundancy, if not coupled with continuous evaluation and adaptation, can lead to complacency and eventual setbacks.

It's easy to fall into this trap. The first step in avoiding it is to recognize the signs early on. This chapter will explore how to detect when you're slipping into complacency and what to do to keep moving forward. As they say, "Don't let the grass grow under your feet". Let's make sure that our success doesn't turn into stagnation.

1.2. Early signs of detecting "You are resting on your Laurels"

Resting on your laurels can happen to anyone after achieving something significant. It's when you start leaning on past victories and stop pushing yourself forward. This happens in sports, business, and life in general. It's like "sitting pretty" after a big win, thinking you've done enough. But resting on past success can lead to a drop in performance, creativity, and growth.

One early sign is avoiding new challenges. If you find yourself sticking to what you know and avoiding risks, it's a red flag. You might also stop learning new things, assuming what got you here will carry you forward. But as the saying goes, "You can't teach an old dog new tricks" - unless, of course, you try. Relying too much on yesterday's victories can cause today's opportunities to slip through your fingers.

In short, don't ***"rest on your laurels"****, k*eep pushing, keep learning, and stay hungry for more. Continuously challenging yourself is essential to sustaining long-term success. Some of the early signs to detect has ***complacency set in***.

You Stop Setting New Goals

One of the most significant indicators that you're ***resting on your laurels*** is when you stop setting new goals. After achieving a major milestone, it's natural to want to take a moment to enjoy your success. However, if that moment turns into a prolonged period without new challenges, it's a red flag.

Samir Aït Saïd, the Algerian Olympic rower, faced a significant setback in his athletic career when he suffered a serious injury just before the

2016 Rio Olympics. His injury was a compound fracture of the tibia and fibula, requiring immediate surgery. Despite the severity of his injury, Aït Saïd remained determined to return to the sport he loved. His resilience and positive attitude became an inspiration to many. Following his recovery, Aït Saïd began training with the goal of competing in the 2020 Tokyo Olympics. His journey back was filled with rigorous rehabilitation, physical therapy, and training to regain his strength and form. Aït Saïd's determination paid off, and he successfully qualified for the Tokyo Olympics.

At the Tokyo Games, Aït Saïd not only competed but also served as a flag bearer for France during the opening ceremony, symbolizing his incredible comeback. Aït Saïd's journey from a horrific injury to competing at the highest level again is a testament to his dedication, resilience, and the power of setting and pursuing goals, even in the face of adversity

You Avoid Taking Risks

Risk-taking is an integral part of growth, and when you start avoiding it, it's often a sign you're **resting on your laurels**. In the early stages of your journey, taking risks feels necessary to break new ground, but once you achieve success, it's tempting to play it safe. After all, why rock the boat when you've already built something great? But, as they say, "nothing ventured, nothing gained." Staying risk-averse can leave you stuck in a rut, preventing further innovation and progress.

The biggest risk is not taking any risk

– Mark Zuckerberg, CEO, Facebook.

Dr. Verghese Kurien, fondly known as the "Father of the White Revolution," exemplified bold leadership and risk-taking. When he launched *Operation Flood*—a groundbreaking initiative aimed at transforming India's dairy industry—he faced immense skepticism and resistance. Yet, Kurien's vision went beyond the status quo. His relentless determination not only made India self-sufficient in milk production but also led to the creation of a cooperative model that empowered millions of rural dairy farmers.

At the core of Kurien's success was his refusal to ***rest on the laurels*** of his earlier achievements. Instead of settling for small gains, he took the bold risk of expanding Amul's model across the country. This transformed a simple cooperative into a global brand synonymous with quality and trust. Had he chosen the comfort of past successes, India's dairy industry might never have experienced the revolution that turned it into the world's largest milk producer.

Kurien's story teaches that real progress lies in continuously pushing boundaries, even in the face of resistance. His vision and refusal to become complacent exemplify what it means to break free from comfort zones and achieve lasting, large-scale impact.

You Feel Overly Comfortable

A classic sign of resting on your laurels is when life starts feeling too comfortable—like a well-worn pair of shoes. Comfort may be enjoyable for a time, but, all good things must come to an end if you want to continue growing. When everything becomes predictable, you might not be pushing yourself enough. In the grand scheme of things, comfort can be a double-edged sword. While it feels safe, it's also a breeding ground for stagnation.

Even in nature, this is evident. Lions in reserves, for example, become comfortable when food is abundant and hunting isn't challenging. Over time, they lose their edge—their hunting skills and stamina start to fade. As the saying goes, "use it or lose it." If these lions were returned to the wild, they might struggle to survive, as their instincts have dulled due to prolonged comfort.

Just like these lions, we humans can find ourselves trapped in our comfort zones, and before we know it, our skills and ambitions may start to atrophy. To avoid this, it's essential to shake things up now and then, step out of the comfort zone, and keep your eyes on the prize.

You Rely Heavily on Past Successes

Do you often find yourself recounting the glory of your past accomplishments? While it's perfectly fine to take pride in your achievements, dwelling on them too much can be a red flag that you're more focused on your past than your future. Success, after all, is not a one-time event, but an ongoing journey. If you're constantly bringing up past victories in conversation or relying on them to define you, it's a sign that you might be stuck in the past. As the saying goes, ***"don't rest on your laurels",*** because what worked yesterday may not serve you tomorrow.

Success is never owned, it's rented, and the rent is due every day
-Rory Vaden, Author.

Take the example of Elvis Presley, often hailed as the "King of Rock and Roll." After an explosive rise to stardom in the 1950s, Presley revolutionized the music industry. However, by the mid-1960s, he was mainly focused on starring in formulaic Hollywood movies and producing soundtracks for those films. This shift towards safe, commercial ventures led to a decline in his musical innovation. During this period, he relied heavily on his past success and image instead of evolving with changing musical trends.

It wasn't until his famous "Comeback Special" in 1968 that Elvis reclaimed his crown by returning to live performances, taking creative risks, and connecting with a new generation of fans. The special allowed him to break free from the stagnation caused by resting on his past successes, reinvigorating his career and reminding the world why he was a musical icon. This move shows that without innovation and a desire to push boundaries, even the greatest stars risk being eclipsed.

Success has destroyed more people, than failures
- Samuel Goldwyn, Producer

In our ever-changing world, relying on past achievements can blind you to new possibilities. If you keep focusing on what you've already done, you might miss out on what you could still achieve. Keep pushing yourself, taking risks, and exploring new directions—because, as Elvis's comeback proved, the only way to stay relevant is to keep moving forward. After all, "a rolling stone gathers no moss." Staying in motion—seeking new challenges and taking risks—is what keeps you sharp, relevant, and ultimately successful in the long run.

You Stop Learning

Another clear sign that you're resting on your laurels is when you stop learning. Lifelong learning is not just a buzzword; it's the fuel for ongoing personal and professional growth. When you feel like you've learned enough, it's a dangerous mindset. "The day you stop learning is the day you stop growing". Learning isn't something you graduate from - it's a continuous process. Just like a plant that stops growing starts dying, your knowledge and skills must constantly be cultivated.

Consider Leonardo da Vinci, the quintessential Renaissance man, who never stopped expanding his knowledge. He wasn't content with being just an extraordinary painter; his curiosity led him to master anatomy, engineering, and countless other fields. Leonardo understood that the pursuit of knowledge is a lifelong endeavour, and this relentless thirst for learning is what made him a genius in so many areas. His life serves as a powerful reminder that innovation and mastery come from constantly evolving, never from standing still.

If you want to stay ahead in your career or personal life, you must actively seek out new knowledge and experiences. Complacency is the enemy of progress. Whether it's reading a new book, taking on a fresh project, or acquiring a new skill, the act of learning keeps you adaptable and primed for the next challenge. As the saying goes, "you're never too old to learn," and the world around you is always changing. To remain competitive and innovative, you have to stay curious and keep growing—because the moment you stop learning is the moment you fall behind.

You Experience a Decline in Passion

Do you remember the fire that once drove you to chase your dreams and achieve your goals? If that passion starts to dim, it's a clear sign you might be **resting on your laurels**. Passion is the fuel that powers ambition, the spark that ignites the pursuit of our dreams, and the force that pushes us to go beyond our limits. But, like a candle left unattended, that passion can burn out over time, leaving behind complacency and routine. When the thrill of tackling challenges fades, and when you start going through the motions rather than striving for new heights, it might mean you've settled into a comfort zone.

A decline in passion manifests in subtle ways at first. You may start to feel detached from your goals, becoming indifferent to tasks that once excited you. A project that used to challenge and inspire you might now feel mundane or tedious. You may stop striving for excellence, falling into the trap of "good enough" and allowing the drive for innovation to fade. The risk here is that without that internal motivation, you lose the edge that once set you apart, risking stagnation instead of continued growth.

Consider Tony Hawk, the legendary skateboarder, whose early career was marked by relentless passion and innovation. Hawk's ambition to push skate boarding's boundaries led him to achieve ground breaking feats, such as landing the first-ever 900-degree spin in competition. His sheer love for the sport was unmistakable. However, as he reached the pinnacle of his career, Hawk began to experience a decline in passion. His focus shifted from pioneering new tricks to preserving his legacy. He no longer felt the same drive to innovate within the competitive skateboarding scene, and his passion seemed to diminish.

Recognizing this shift, Hawk took steps to rekindle his enthusiasm by embracing fresh challenges. He poured his energy into launching the wildly successful Tony Hawk's Pro Skater video game series, which not only revitalized his passion but also introduced skateboarding to a new generation of fans. Hawk also became involved in philanthropic efforts and youth skateboarding programs, reigniting his love for the sport through its positive impact on young skaters. His journey demonstrates that even the most accomplished individuals can experience a drop in passion, but with the right mindset, they can rediscover it in new ventures and challenges.

Hawk's story is a reminder that passion needs nurturing, just like any other part of life. If you find yourself losing interest in what once made you excited, it's important to seek out new sources of inspiration and push yourself outside of your comfort zone. "You can't burn the candle at both ends," but you can always relight it with a fresh spark.

You Surround Yourself with Sycophants

Another sign of resting on your laurels is when you surround yourself with people who never challenge you—people who agree with everything you say or constantly praise your past achievements without encouraging you to reach higher. These sycophants can make life easier in the short term, but their presence often stifles growth and innovation in the long run. When you only hear what you want to hear, you're left without critical feedback that can help you identify blind spots or areas that need improvement. Without the "iron sharpens iron" dynamic, it becomes easier to become complacent and ignore emerging challenges. This dynamic can be dangerous, particularly for leaders. A leader who surrounds themselves with only agreeable voices risks overlooking critical issues or failing to recognize shifts in the landscape, which can lead to significant problems down the road. History is filled with examples of leaders who were brought down because they were too insulated by sycophants to make informed decisions. "Too many cooks may spoil the broth," but too few perspectives can make you blind to the mistakes that need correcting.

One company that has tackled this issue head-on is Bridgewater Associates, the global hedge fund led by Ray Dalio. Bridgewater is famous for its policy of "radical transparency," where open criticism and feedback are encouraged regardless of rank. Almost all meetings are recorded, and employees are expected to speak their minds and challenge each other's ideas. This culture of transparency ensures that decisions are made based on merit rather than flattery, and the presence of yes-men is minimized. By fostering an environment where critical thinking and openness are valued, Bridgewater reduces the risks associated with resting on past successes and encourages continuous improvement.

Surrounding yourself with "yes" people might feel comfortable, but it ultimately leads to complacency. To grow and continue achieving, you need a team that challenges you, provides honest feedback, and helps push you toward new goals.

You Ignore Next Generation Talent

Ignoring the development and inclusion of next-generation talent is a significant sign that you may be *resting on your laurels*. When you become complacent in your success, there's a tendency to focus solely on the present, overlooking the importance of cultivating the future leaders and innovators who will carry your legacy forward. Next-generation talent often comes with a different set of skills, knowledge of new technologies, and innovative ideas that can drive growth. Ignoring this talent pool can lead to missed opportunities for innovation and adaptation. Consider the tech industry, where rapid advancements are the norm. Companies that fail to engage with and nurture young talent often struggle to keep up with technological changes and market demands.

Google implemented a policy where employees could spend 20% of their work time on projects they were passionate about, even if those projects were outside of their regular job responsibilities. This strategy encouraged innovation and led to the creation of several successful products, including Gmail and Google News. Not only did this policy allow the company to capitalize on new ideas, but it also empowered young talent to contribute to the company's success and future direction. This illustrates how organizations can benefit from giving the next generation room to grow and innovate, rather than letting them remain in the shadows. This approach not only fosters creativity but also inspires the next generation of tech innovators to think beyond their job descriptions.

You Stop Seeking New Ideas

One of the surest signs of complacency is when you or your team stops seeking out new ideas. Organizations that were once driven by innovation and forward-thinking may begin to rest on their laurels, relying on the success of existing products or processes. This shift often happens gradually—at first, you might feel that you've "figured it out," and there's no need to fix what isn't broken. But over time, this mindset stifles creativity and limits opportunities for growth. When the hunger for new ideas fades, it's usually a sign that comfort has taken over.

For instance, if a company becomes too reliant on past successes and avoids experimenting with new technologies or market approaches, they risk becoming irrelevant. Consider Kodak, which was a dominant player in the photography industry but failed to embrace digital technology despite pioneering it. While it was riding high on the profits from its traditional film business, the company didn't invest in digital photography's future ultimately leading to its downfall. By the time Kodak recognized the shift, it was too late, and they were left behind as newer players like Canon, Nikon, and digital startups flourished.

This is why companies must avoid falling into the trap of relying on past glory and consistently strive to explore new ideas. When organizations encourage employees at all levels—especially the younger, tech-savvy generation—to bring forth their innovative thinking, they not only foster a culture of continuous improvement but also position themselves to adapt to market demands. After all, we can certainly embrace the wisdom of younger generations who have their fingers on the pulse of tomorrow's trends.

We cannot solve problems with the same thinking we used when we created them.

-Albert Einstein, Scientist

P&G's "Connect + Develop" program is a well-known example of open innovation in action. The company recognized that to stay competitive and continue to innovate at scale, it needed to tap into external ideas and expertise. Instead of relying solely on its internal R&D department, P&G actively seeks ideas from external partners, startups, inventors, and entrepreneurs. This approach not only accelerates the pace of innovation but also broadens the scope of possible solutions. The core of the

"Connect + Develop" program is its collaboration with a network of over 2,000 external partners, ranging from research institutes and suppliers to individual inventors and small startups. This partnership network helps P&G fill gaps in its internal capabilities by identifying new technologies and products that can be adapted and integrated into P&G's product lines.

A notable success from this program is the Swiffer cleaning products line, which originated from external collaboration. P&G identified a gap in their internal solutions and, by working with external inventors, was able to quickly bring the Swiffer to market, which became a major success globally.

The program's openness enables P&G to tap into innovation across various domains while still maintaining a strong internal research and development team to ensure product quality and relevance. This blending of external ideas with internal expertise helps P&G stay agile and innovate across categories.

IBM, a global leader in technology, takes a different yet equally effective approach with its "Idea Jam" strategy. IBM employs a collaborative, crowdsourcing model where employees, partners, and even customers come together in a structured, online brainstorming session. These "Idea Jams" are designed to generate a wide range of innovative ideas in a short amount of time by leveraging the collective intelligence of diverse stakeholders.

An Idea Jam typically lasts for a set period, such as 72 hours, during which participants contribute and evaluate ideas in real time. These sessions foster a democratic and inclusive approach to problem-solving, as anyone involved can voice their opinions or suggest improvements. The crowdsourcing aspect helps IBM identify and refine ideas that may not have surfaced in a traditional top-down innovation model.

For example, through its Idea Jams, IBM has successfully addressed pressing business challenges, created new services, and launched product innovations. The Smarter Planet initiative, which promotes technologies that help make systems and infrastructure more intelligent, was significantly influenced by ideas generated from IBM's Idea Jam sessions.

By encouraging contributions from a wide range of stakeholders, IBM ensures that innovation happens not just within its corporate walls but through a broader, more inclusive network. This process helps IBM remain at the forefront of the rapidly changing tech landscape.

You Stop Seeking Feedback

When you stop seeking feedback, you close off one of the most vital avenues for growth and improvement. Feedback offers fresh perspectives and uncovers blind spots that may hinder your progress. Yet, when resting on past achievements, it's easy to become resistant to feedback, viewing it as unnecessary or irrelevant. This avoidance can be particularly damaging in leadership roles, where a lack of constructive criticism from colleagues or team members can stifle innovation and problem-solving. Surrounding yourself with "yes-men" — people who only agree with you — can lead to a dangerous echo chamber, where only positive reinforcement is heard, and critical opportunities for growth are missed.

Johari Window

The Johari Window, created by psychologists Joseph Luft and Harrington Ingham in 1955, is a tool to enhance self-awareness and interpersonal relationships. It is widely used in self-help groups and workplaces to foster trust, communication, and personal growth. The Johari Window model can further highlight the importance of feedback by illustrating how self-awareness is divided into four quadrants: the "open area" (what you and others know about yourself), the "blind area" (what others see but you are unaware of), the "hidden area" (what you know but others don't), and the "unknown area" (what neither you nor others are aware of). Feedback plays a crucial role in reducing the size of the "blind area," giving you insights into aspects of yourself or your leadership that you may overlook. Without feedback, your blind spots remain unchallenged, which can limit both personal and organizational growth.

A practical tool that combats this complacency is the "Start, Stop, Continue" feedback model. This model, used by companies like Netflix, organizes feedback into three actionable categories: what you should **start** doing, **stop** doing, and **continue** doing. This structure makes

16

feedback clear and actionable, ensuring that individuals or organizations can make meaningful adjustments to their practices and remain adaptive in a changing environment.

You Resist Change

Another clear sign of complacency is resistance to change. When past success leads to a sense of comfort, change is often seen as an unnecessary risk or a burden. However, innovation thrives on adaptability. Companies and individuals that resist change, especially in a rapidly evolving marketplace, often find themselves falling behind. New technologies, industry trends, or shifts in consumer behavior are essential drivers of progress. A strong example from China's manufacturing industry in the 1980s involves Shougang Group, one of China's largest steel producers. During this period, the company struggled with outdated production methods and resistance to adopting new technologies, similar to how Kodak missed the digital revolution. Chinese manufacturing was primarily state-controlled, and many companies, like Shougang, relied on traditional methods that had brought them success in the past. However, as global competition increased and technological advancements transformed the industry, companies that did not adapt quickly fell behind.

Shougang, at first, was slow to innovate, missing opportunities to modernize its factories and streamline production processes. It resisted adopting automation technologies and more efficient steelmaking methods that competitors in Japan and South Korea were embracing. As a result, Shougang faced declining competitiveness and profitability. It wasn't until the 1990s, when the company embraced reforms, invested in new technology, and relocated its operations to improve environmental impact and efficiency, that it regained its footing.

This shift highlights the importance of adaptability in a fast-changing world. Like many manufacturers of the 1980s, Shougang initially resisted change, but its eventual pivot toward innovation allowed it to survive and thrive in a more competitive global marketplace.

In today's world, the lesson from Shougang is clear: clinging to past successes and resisting change can lead to stagnation, while embracing innovation and adaptability is crucial for long-term growth and survival.

Adaptability in today's world is not just a virtue; it's a necessity for survival. By welcoming change, whether through adopting new technologies or embracing new ideas, you open the door to continuous improvement and long-term success.

It is not the strongest of the species that survive, nor the most intelligent, but the one most adaptable to change.

-Charles Darwin

Your Behaviour Becomes Arrogant

When success takes hold, it can sometimes lead to a subtle shift in behavior, where confidence starts to evolve into arrogance. This is a dangerous transformation because arrogance often blinds you to the need for growth and improvement. Like the saying goes, "pride comes before a fall," and this change in attitude can become an early warning sign that you're ***resting on your laurels***. The key problem with arrogance is that it shuts down the humility necessary for learning and adapting to new challenges.

Arrogance tends to creep into your interactions with others. You might begin to feel that your way of doing things is the only correct approach, and this attitude leads you to dismiss the ideas, opinions, or contributions of others as less valuable. This kind of behaviour doesn't just damage relationships — it can also create a toxic work environment where people feel stifled. When innovation is smothered because employees are too afraid to speak up or challenge ideas, the very collaboration and openness that may have once fuelled your success disappear, replaced by rigid hierarchy.

Netflix, for instance, has famously taken a stand against this kind of toxic behavior with its "No Brilliant Jerks" policy. In this company, no matter how talented or successful an individual may be, if they disrupt teamwork or exhibit arrogance, they are shown the door. Netflix values a team-oriented culture over individual heroics, recognizing that innovation thrives when egos are kept in check. This policy ensures that arrogance doesn't take root and that sycophants don't wield undue influence. Instead, it promotes a culture of mutual respect where ideas are openly shared, and every voice matters.

By maintaining this balanced approach, Netflix has managed to curb the influence of arrogance, ensuring that no one, no matter how brilliant, "gets too big for their boots". It's a reminder that even after great success, staying humble and fostering teamwork are essential for continued growth and innovation.

You Become Indiscipline and Less Punctual

Success can sometimes breed a sense of complacency, leading to a decline in discipline and punctuality. When you start resting on your laurels, the rigor and routine that once drove you to achieve your goals may begin to slip. This is a subtle but telling sign that you are no longer striving for excellence with the same intensity as before.

Indiscipline and a lack of punctuality can manifest in various aspects of your life. Meetings that you once attended on time may start to feel less urgent, deadlines that were previously non-negotiable might begin to feel flexible, and the structured approach that helped you succeed could give way to a more casual attitude. The saying "you reap what you sow" comes to mind—if you let your discipline slide, it won't be long before the results reflect that.

This shift often stems from a belief that your previous achievements afford you the luxury of relaxation and that the same level of effort is no longer necessary.

You Rely Too Much on Your Reputation

Relying too heavily on your reputation can be a double-edged sword. When you've achieved a certain level of success, it's natural to feel confident in the recognition and respect you've earned. However, this confidence can become a trap if it leads you to believe that your reputation alone is enough to sustain your success.

Over time, you might start to put less effort into your work, assuming that your past achievements will continue to speak for themselves. This mindset can result in a decline in the quality of your output. Clients, colleagues, or customers who once admired your work may begin to notice a drop in standards, leading to dissatisfaction and a tarnished reputation.

For instance, consider the case of a once-renowned author who stops refining their craft, assuming that their name alone will ensure book sales. Eventually, readers may lose interest as the quality of the books declines, leading to a decrease in sales and a loss of credibility. In the business world, companies that *rest on their laurels* and rely solely on their brand name, without continuing to innovate or improve, often find themselves outpaced by more agile and forward-thinking competitors.

Maintaining discipline and punctuality, even after reaching your goals, keeps you sharp and prevents complacency from taking root. As the idiom goes, "old habits die hard," but this can work both ways - if you allow poor habits to develop, they'll be just as hard to break as the good ones once were.

You Rely on the Same Strategies

Success often leads to a reliance on strategies that worked in the past, but what worked yesterday may not work today. If you find yourself continually using the same approaches without adapting to new challenges, you're likely resting on your laurels. For instance, a marketing team that sticks to outdated campaigns because they were successful years ago might miss out on engaging with modern audiences. Innovation requires constant adaptation, and sticking to old strategies can lead to irrelevance.

The greatest danger in times of turbulence is not the turbulence; it is to act with yesterday's logic.

-Peter Drucker, Management Consultant

In sports, success often requires adaptation, especially as new challenges arise and competition evolves. A prime example of an athlete who changed his strategy to achieve further success is Michael Jordan, one of the greatest basketball players of all time.

During the early years of his career, Jordan was known for his incredible athleticism, speed, and scoring ability. His game was largely focused on driving to the basket, utilizing his explosiveness to outscore his opponents. However, as he aged, his physical abilities began to wane. Rather than relying on the same approach that had made him successful in his younger years, Jordan adapted his game to remain competitive.

In the latter part of his career, Jordan developed one of the most effective mid-range jump shots in NBA history. He shifted from relying solely on his athleticism to honing a more skillful, tactical game. This adaptation not only prolonged his career but also helped him win three more NBA championships with the Chicago Bulls after his first retirement.

Jordan's ability to evolve his game, shifting from an aggressive, physically dominant style to a more strategic, skill-based approach, is a testament to his adaptability. By recognizing that what had worked for him earlier in his career was no longer enough, he embraced new strategies that kept him at the top of the sport.

This example illustrates the importance of continuously reassessing and adapting strategies, even in the face of past success. As the competitive environment changes, innovation and evolution become critical to maintaining relevance and achieving sustained success. Sticking to the same strategies can quickly lead to irrelevance, like "flogging a dead horse." To stay competitive, businesses and individuals alike need to adapt to new realities, embracing change rather than resisting it.

You Start Neglecting Relationships and Responsibilities

When success goes to your head, it's easy to start neglecting important relationships and responsibilities. This can lead to the classic case of "biting the hand that feeds you," where you forget the contributions of others who helped you rise. Success can sometimes lead to a sense of self-sufficiency, where you feel that you no longer need the input or support of others. This sense of independence can be empowering, but it can also lead to isolation a dangerous state where you stop seeking the opinions, advice, or companionship of others. A complacent person may stop engaging with their team or peers, assuming that their leadership or role is secure and that they don't need to invest in relationships.

When you isolate yourself, you may begin to believe that you know best in all situations, disregarding the value that diverse perspectives can bring. Isolation can also create tunnel vision, where you start to believe "my way or the highway" is the best and only path forward. This can result in a narrow-minded approach to problem-solving and decision-making, where you miss out on innovative ideas and critical feedback that could help you grow. Over time, this isolation can create a disconnect between you and your team, peers, or audience, leading to a lack of collaboration and a stagnation in your work.

For example, a successful leader who becomes isolated might stop consulting with their team, believing they have all the answers. This can lead to decisions that are out of touch with the reality on the ground, causing frustration among team members and ultimately harming the organization's progress.

You Enter into Early Retirement Mode

As individuals become satisfied with their past accomplishments, they might begin to disengage from their professional responsibilities. This could manifest as a reduced drive to take on new challenges or a reluctance to learn new skills, leading to a decline in their pursuit of career advancement. This can be akin to "putting the cart before the horse," assuming that past success guarantees future relevance. The individual might believe they've "paid their dues" and are entitled to relax, justifying a shift from professional ambition to personal satisfaction. Essentially, they may feel they've "earned the right" to coast on previous successes, leading to a gradual withdrawal from the active pursuit of professional growth. When someone is ***resting on their laurels***, there is often a shift in focus from professional ambition to personal satisfaction. This can include spending more time on hobbies, travel, or family activities, often at the expense of their work. The individual may justify this shift by believing their previous achievements have afforded them the luxury to prioritize leisure, signaling a transition into a retirement mindset. This early retirement mode can also foster complacency. An individual may feel they have "earned the right to relax" and stop pushing for professional growth, assuming that their earlier accomplishments have given them a free pass to slow down.

In Japan, the official retirement age is often around 60-65, but many retirees continue working in some capacity after reaching this age. This is partly due to financial necessity, as the public pension system may not fully cover living expenses, but also due to cultural factors. Work is highly valued in Japanese society, and many older adults choose to continue working to stay active and maintain a sense of purpose. Japan has a system known as "re-employment" (*saikoyou*), where companies rehire retired employees, often in part-time or contract positions. These "silver" jobs, named for the senior population they are designed for, allow older workers to stay engaged in the workforce while potentially reducing their hours or responsibilities. This practice is supported by government policies encouraging companies to retain older workers. Culturally, there is a strong emphasis on the value of contributing to society, regardless of age. Retirement in Japan doesn't always imply a cessation of work but rather a transition to a different type of work or role. The concept of "IKIGAI", which refers to a sense of purpose or reason for being, plays a significant role in how the elderly approach retirement. Many continue to work or volunteer to fulfill their IKIGAI.

John B. Goodenough, the Nobel Prize-winning physicist known for his work in developing the lithium-ion battery, has been quoted on retirement, reflecting his philosophy of lifelong learning and contribution. John B. Goodenough once said, "If one retires, it doesn't mean he should just wait to die." This quote reflects his belief that retirement should not signify the end of a meaningful life. Instead, it should be an opportunity to continue contributing, learning, and staying active. Goodenough's perspective underscores the importance of maintaining purpose and engagement, regardless of age or official retirement status.

The normal age of Nobel Prize winners varies across categories and historical periods, but a common observation is that many laureates are often in their 50s or 60s when they receive the award. This age range reflects the culmination of years of dedicated work, research, and significant contributions in their respective fields. Roger Penrose was 89 years old when he received the Nobel prize for his work on black holes and general relativity. James Peebles was 77 years old when he received Nobel Prize for his theoretical discoveries in physical cosmology.

Your Personality is Transformed

Complacency can manifest through various signs in the personality. This includes excessive anger, reduced resistance to challenges, irritation, and a loss of interest. When someone becomes complacent, they might experience frustration and anger if forced out of their comfort zone or faced with demands that disrupt their perceived status quo. This anger often arises from resistance to change. Complacency also leads to a lack of resistance, where the individual may stop challenging themselves or others, accepting lower standards and becoming passive. Irritation can occur when complacent individuals are confronted with tasks or responsibilities, they no longer feel motivated to address, especially if reminded of their declining performance. Furthermore, a significant loss of interest in both work and personal relationships can be a "red flag," pointing to a deeper stagnation. These changes reflect more than just complacency; they can also indicate burnout or other mental health concerns. While these signs are indicative of complacency, they may also signal other issues such as burnout, stress, or mental health concerns, highlighting the importance of considering the broader context when evaluating these behaviours.

When employees accept a golden handshake, their behavioural changes can include increased anger, irritation, and a loss of interest in their remaining work or responsibilities. This transition often brings about feelings of frustration, especially if the employee perceives the handshake as a forced exit rather than a voluntary choice. As they prepare to leave, they may experience heightened irritation due to the abrupt end of their career and the potential disruption of their professional identity. This irritation can be directed towards remaining tasks, colleagues, or the organization itself.

You Start Procrastinating

When complacency sets in, procrastination often follows as a subtle but telling sign. You start delaying important tasks, convincing yourself that there's plenty of time, or that your previous accomplishments give you a buffer to coast for a while. This mindset leads to a dangerous cycle where the urgency and discipline that fueled your earlier success fade, and you find yourself continually postponing actions that are crucial to progress. Imagine a successful entrepreneur who built a thriving startup. After hitting significant revenue milestones and gaining industry recognition, they begin to put off working on new product developments or exploring emerging markets, thinking their current success will carry them forward. Meetings to brainstorm fresh ideas or finalize expansion strategies get delayed, and crucial decisions are deferred. The entrepreneur may rationalize these delays by saying they're "taking a well-deserved break" or "waiting for the right time," but in reality, they're allowing their momentum to slip. Over time, competitors might catch up, and the once-innovative company risks falling behind, all because of procrastination fuelled by resting on past achievements.

You Start Giving a Lot of Advices

One of the early signs of resting on your laurels is that you begin giving a lot of unsolicited advice. This behaviour can often stem from a sense of self-satisfaction with past achievements, making you believe that your experiences have made you an authority on various topics. While it's natural to want to share what you've learned, giving too much advice can indicate complacency. It definitely glorifies your past but you forgot to actively seeking new challenges.

When someone starts dishing out advice left, right, and center, it may signal that they've stopped pushing themselves and are instead basking in the glow of their former accomplishments. In other words, they may be *resting on their laurels,* like an old sailor telling tales of past voyages instead of setting sail on new adventures.

Over time, this habit of giving too much advice may turn from helpful to condescending. If you constantly tell others how they should handle things, you might come across as thinking you're always right - a form of arrogance. As the saying goes, "actions speak louder than words". Instead of just advising others, demonstrating that you're still learning and growing shows much more about your character and adaptability.

Moreover, offering advice without walking the talk may create friction with colleagues or peers, especially when it seems you're avoiding fresh challenges yourself. This can lead to "biting off more than you can chew", as your credibility diminishes when people realize you're leaning more on past successes than actively engaging in the present.

You Want Instant Gratification

Instant gratification has increasingly become a trap for the current generation, affecting not just productivity but creativity and the value of hard work. With everything available at our fingertips whether it's streaming movies on-demand, receiving instant social media feedback, or ordering products online with next-day delivery our ability to wait for results is diminishing. This constant cycle of quick rewards, while convenient, often comes at a cost: it kills the motivation to engage in deep, meaningful work and undermines the patience required for creative breakthroughs.

Creativity thrives in environments where individuals take time to think, experiment, fail, and try again. However, the immediate dopamine hit from likes, views, or fast solutions has conditioned many to expect instant results, without the effort or failure necessary to foster creativity. For instance, writing a novel, composing music, or mastering a craft takes countless hours of practice and revision. When people prioritize fast validation, they often give up when faced with challenges, missing the opportunity for true creative growth.

The pursuit of instant gratification can also erode the work ethic. Instead of putting in the time and effort to learn difficult skills or solve complex problems, many opt for shortcuts or easy rewards, leading to complacency. This can result in a lack of resilience and persistence, essential traits for achieving long-term goals. The constant allure of immediate rewards can rob individuals of the joy of deep work the kind of focused, sustained effort that leads to innovation, self-mastery, and truly significant accomplishments.

For example, platforms providing one minute video, can be fun but often divert attention from more substantive tasks. Studies have shown that excessive reliance on instant rewards can lower attention spans and reduce the ability to engage in tasks that require patience and prolonged effort. People may stop pursuing creative projects or ambitious goals because they don't see immediate results, which ultimately stifles growth and limits potential.

To combat this, it's essential to reconnect with the value of delayed gratification. Success and creativity take time, effort, and resilience. By stepping away from the lure of instant rewards and focusing on long-term goals, we can rediscover the power of hard work, creativity, and perseverance—skills that lead to lasting success and deeper fulfilment.

You are Facing Excessive Competition

Excessive competition can lead to both burnout and complacency, creating a paradox in which individuals or organizations either overextend themselves or, conversely, stop striving altogether. While healthy competition can drive innovation and performance, an overly competitive environment can foster a short-sighted mentality. People begin to prioritize winning at all costs, often adopting quick-fix strategies just to stay ahead of rivals, rather than focusing on long-term growth, creativity, or collaboration.

On the flip side, once certain individuals or organizations achieve their goals, they can fall into complacency. The comfort of success leads them to *rest on their laurels*, believing that past achievements are sufficient to sustain future success. For example, an athlete who wins several championships may reduce their training intensity, believing they've reached the pinnacle of their career. This mindset leaves them vulnerable to more motivated, up-and-coming competitors.

In corporate environments, excessive competition can stifle creativity as companies focus solely on outperforming rivals rather than fostering a culture of innovation. Once a dominant market position is secured, complacency can creep in, with the company failing to adapt to new trends or technologies, eventually being overtaken by more agile competitors. This has been seen in industries ranging from technology to retail, where major players, once at the top, were outpaced by more innovative challengers who weren't bogged down by complacency.

Balancing competition with the pursuit of growth and continuous improvement is crucial to avoid both burnout and the pitfalls of complacency.

Your Alcohol Consumption Escalates

For individuals who have achieved significant success, there may be a tendency to *rest on their laurels* and become complacent. This complacency can lead to a lack of fulfilment or boredom, which may drive some to increasingly rely on alcohol as a means of coping. Initially, drinking may serve as a reward or a way to relax, but over time, it can escalate into a dependency that masks deeper issues, such as the fear of facing new challenges or the discomfort of potential failure. As someone rests on their laurels, they might begin to neglect their professional or personal responsibilities, assuming that their past achievements will continue to carry them forward. Alcohol abuse exacerbates this neglect, as the individual may increasingly prioritize drinking over maintaining their standards of performance. This neglect not only undermines their reputation and relationships but also perpetuates a cycle where they rely on past successes to justify their current lack of engagement.

You Start Giving Excuses

One of the most signs of complacency is when you start giving excuses for poor performance or missed opportunities. At first, these excuses may seem harmless—little justifications you tell yourself to make sense of why things didn't go as planned. But slowly, these excuses pile up, and before you know it, they become a protective shield against confronting the harsh reality: you've grown too comfortable, and you're afraid to push the boundaries any further.

The moment you start shifting the blame, you've entered dangerous territory. It's a subtle but significant shift from owning your failures to rationalizing them. When you're on top of your game, you take responsibility for setbacks and use them as a catalyst for growth. But as soon as you start giving excuses, you begin insulating yourself from criticism both external and internal. It becomes easier to explain away why things aren't going well rather than taking action to change them.

At first, the excuses might seem justified. "I was too busy with other projects," or "This year has been exceptionally challenging". These are common refrains that all of us use from time to time. But the problem arises when these explanations become habitual. The moment you start looking outward rather than inward, you start creating a narrative that protects your ego but prevents growth.

Consider the case of a top athlete who, after achieving a major victory, begins to coast. Let's say they start losing matches or falling short in competitions. Instead of looking at how their training has faltered or how their strategy needs updating, they might start blaming external factors: "The referee made bad calls," "My opponent got lucky," or "The conditions were unfavorable". These excuses may shield the athlete from the pain of failure, but they also prevent them from making the necessary adjustments to reclaim their spot at the top.

This phenomenon is especially dangerous because the more you rely on excuses, the easier it becomes to make them. It's a slippery slope. What starts as a single instance of rationalizing can quickly spiral into a mindset where you consistently avoid taking responsibility. This, in turn, can lead to stagnation and, ultimately, decline. It's the classic case of "resting on your laurels"—you become so focused on defending your past success that you stop striving for future achievements.

Excuses also stifle creativity and innovation. When you convince yourself that external factors are to blame, you stop looking for new ways to overcome challenges. You're no longer in problem-solving mode but rather in defense mode, protecting your ego and your reputation. This is where complacency becomes particularly dangerous because it halts progress entirely. If you're constantly rationalizing why things aren't working, you're not exploring new ideas, taking risks, or seeking growth.

You Have Earned a Lot

While financial success can bring comfort, security, and freedom, it can also, paradoxically, be a breeding ground for complacency. The more money one accumulates, the greater the risk of becoming disconnected from the drive and hunger that originally fueled that success. Excessive wealth, if not managed with the right mindset, can slowly erode ambition, risk-taking, and innovation.

When people achieve significant financial success, they often experience a sense of arrival. After years of hard work and dedication, it's tempting to believe they've earned the right to "relax" and enjoy their wealth. While taking time to celebrate achievements is crucial, excessive money can lull people into a false sense of security where they stop pushing boundaries, stop seeking growth, and start resting on their laurels.

Financial abundance often provides a cushion that allows individuals to avoid risks. In the absence of financial pressure, there's little urgency to innovate or take on new challenges. This comfort can lead to inertia, where people become risk-averse and overly protective of their existing assets. Rather than striving for more, they become content with maintaining what they already have, even if it means stagnating.

Your Tongue Turns Bitter

One sign you might be resting on your laurels is when you start feeling bitter or resentful toward others' successes or fresh ideas. You might catch yourself thinking, *Why are they getting so much attention? What's so special about that?* Instead of celebrating their growth or learning from their achievements, you dismiss them or feel irritated. This bitterness often comes from a deeper place—it's not really about them; it's about you. Maybe you've stopped challenging yourself, and their progress reminds you of what you're not doing. This bitterness often isn't about them at all—it's about you. It's a subtle, internal frustration, stemming from the realization that you've stopped pushing yourself forward.

Imagine being the star of the show for years, basking in applause and admiration, and then watching someone else take the spotlight with a new act. Instead of clapping for them, you sit back, arms crossed, thinking about how your old performance was better. But deep down, the irritation comes from knowing you haven't updated your act in a while. This bitterness can be a powerful mirror, reflecting a need for growth and new challenges. It's a quiet alarm bell telling you to stop looking back and start moving forward again. Recognizing this is the first step to breaking free and reigniting your own journey toward progress. Bitterness is a subtle but powerful signal—it's your mind nudging you to ask, *Am I really giving my best right now?* It's not a dead end; it's an opportunity to pause, reflect, and reignite your own drive. Instead of resenting others, use their success as a spark to light your own fire again. Remember, your growth doesn't stop just because you've succeeded once—there's always another summit to climb.

1.3. Understanding the Comfort Zone

Imagine waking up one morning to find that everything you've worked for, everything you've built, is starting to slip away. Not because of a sudden disaster or a fierce competitor, but because of something much more insidious—something that crept in quietly, unnoticed, and took root while you were basking in the glow of your past achievements.

Comfort is the worst addiction – Marcus Aurelius

This is the story of Sarah, a highly successful entrepreneur who had it all: a thriving business, industry accolades, and financial security. She was the definition of success, admired by her peers and envied by her competitors. But what no one knew, not even Sarah herself, was that her greatest threat wasn't external. It wasn't a new competitor or a market downturn. It was the subtle but dangerous force of complacency.

The downfall started very slowly. A few missed opportunities here, a lack of urgency there. "We've got this," she told herself. After all, her company had been the leader in its field for years. What could possibly go wrong?

But as weeks turned into months, those small lapses began to compound. New competitors entered the market, hungrier and more innovative. Customers started drifting away, lured by fresher ideas and better solutions. Sarah's once-unshakable confidence began to waver as she realized something was terribly wrong.

What had happened? How did a business that was once unstoppable begin to falter? The answer was simple yet profound: Sarah had unknowingly fallen into the trap of resting on her laurels. She had allowed her past successes to lull her into a false sense of security, forgetting that in a world that never stops evolving, standing still is the same as moving backward.

We all know that feeling. The sense of security that comes when you've finally made it—whether it's landing your dream job, reaching a milestone in your career, or achieving a personal goal. You've worked hard to get here, and now you're enjoying the fruits of your labor. It feels good, doesn't it? But here's the catch: while comfort feels nice, it can also be the very thing that holds you back.

The comfort zone is a psychological state where you feel safe, in control, and free from stress. It's a place where everything is familiar, and there's little to no risk involved. While it's natural to want to stay in this zone, doing so can trap you, preventing you from growing and reaching your full potential. It is just like we want to travel every day on the same path we know rather exploring new path.

The concept of the comfort zone was first popularized by psychologist Alasdair A. K. White in 2009. White explained that people operate within a space where their anxiety is low and they feel in control. This is the comfort zone. When individuals step outside this zone, they enter a state of increased anxiety and stress, but also of heightened performance. This is known as the "optimal performance zone" **(White, 2009).**

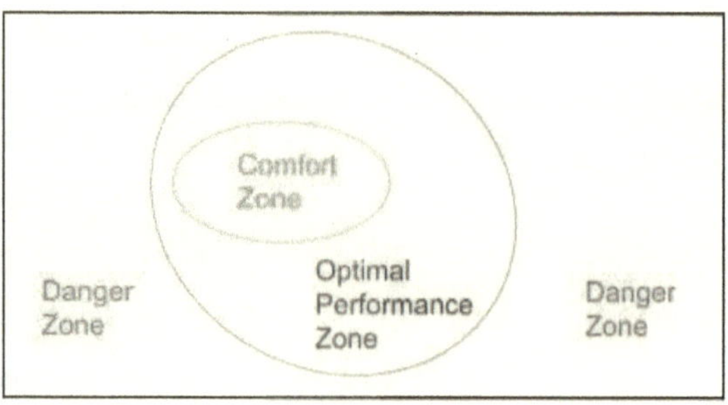

Comfort Zone Model (White, 2009)

White's theory suggests that while staying within the comfort zone might lead to steady, predictable outcomes, it's only by stepping into the optimal performance zone that individuals can achieve peak performance and personal growth.

1.4. The Risks of Staying in Your Comfort Zone

The comfort zone feels good because it's safe. Within this zone, the brain conserves energy by relying on established routines and habits. You don't need to expend much mental effort because you're operating on autopilot. There's no fear of failure because you're not taking any risks.

However, this safety comes at a cost. When you stay in your comfort zone for too long, you stop challenging yourself. You become stagnant. And in a world, that's constantly changing, stagnation is a risk you can't afford to take.

Consider a professional athlete who has reached the top of their game. They've mastered their sport, won multiple championships, and are at the peak of their career. It's tempting for them to keep doing what they've always done because it's worked so well in the past. But the moment they stop pushing themselves to improve, their performance begins to decline. Younger, hungrier athletes, who are still striving to break out of their comfort zones, quickly rise to the top, leaving the complacent athlete behind.

This isn't just true in sports. In business, technology, and even personal relationships, staying in the comfort zone can lead to missed opportunities, unfulfilled potential, and ultimately, failure.

The Yerkes-Dodson Law provides valuable insight into the relationship between stress (or arousal) and performance, emphasizing the importance of balance. Initially developed by psychologists Robert M. Yerkes and John D. Dodson in 1908, this law posits that as arousal levels increase, performance tends to improve—but only to a certain point. Beyond this optimal level of stress, additional arousal begins to impair performance. This phenomenon can be visualized as an inverted U-shaped curve, where moderate stress leads to peak performance, but excessive stress causes a decline in effectiveness.

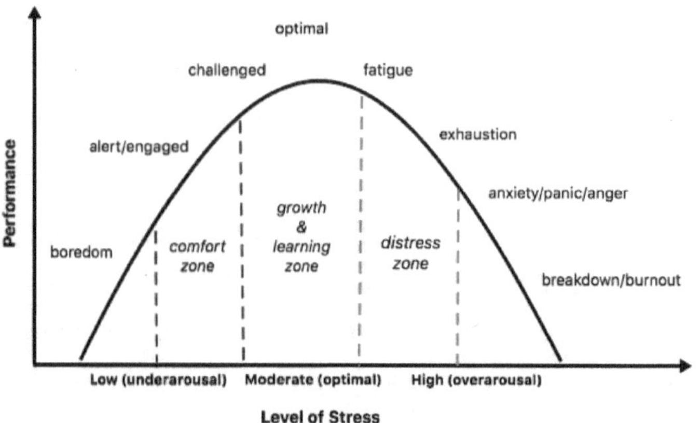

Yerkes-Dodson Law

At the lower end of the curve, insufficient arousal such as boredom or lack of challenge results in underperformance because the individual is not stimulated enough to focus or push themselves. In contrast, at the upper end of the curve, too much arousal leads to anxiety, overwhelm, and a breakdown in performance. Thus, the Yerkes-Dodson Law explains why both comfort and excessive stress can hinder growth and performance.

For instance, imagine a student preparing for an important exam. If they feel too comfortable and relaxed, they may not put in the necessary effort, resulting in subpar preparation and poor performance. However, if they are overly stressed and anxious, the pressure can cloud their thinking and ability to retain information. The sweet spot lies in moderate stress—enough to push them to focus and challenge themselves, but not so much that it causes panic or paralysis.

The Yerkes-Dodson Law also applies to broader contexts, such as professional development or leadership roles. When individuals remain in their comfort zones for too long, complacency can set in, leading to stagnation and lacklustre performance. On the other hand, pushing beyond the comfort zone—by taking on new challenges, responsibilities, or skill sets—introduces a moderate level of stress that can drive growth, innovation, and higher achievement.

However, it's crucial to recognize that too much stress, particularly chronic or extreme, can backfire, leading to burnout, decreased mental health, and diminished productivity. This is why striking the right balance between challenge and relaxation is essential for sustainable growth, whether in personal life, academics, or the workplace.

In practice, the Yerkes-Dodson Law serves as a reminder that growth requires stepping outside the comfort zone, but also that maintaining a healthy relationship with stress is key to unlocking one's full potential.

1.5. Escape the Shackles of Comfort Zone

So, how do you escape the comfort zone trap? The first step is awareness. Notice when you're stuck in a routine, immediately challenge yourself to try something new. Start with small steps - take on a new project at work, learn a new skill, or set a challenging personal goal. The more you practice stepping outside your comfort zone, the easier it becomes.

Here are some practical strategies to help you break free the shackles of comfort zone:

Reframe Success as a Journey, Not a Destination

To sustain progress, it's crucial to adopt a perspective that views success as a continuous journey rather than a static endpoint. Carol Dweck's research on the "growth mindset" emphasizes the importance of embracing challenges, learning from failures, and recognizing that talents and abilities can be developed over time. In her book, *Mindset: The New Psychology of Success* (2006), Dweck contrasts the growth mindset with a fixed mindset, where individuals believe their skills and intelligence are static and cannot be improved. Those with a fixed mindset may see failure as a reflection of their limitations, while those with a growth mindset view it as an opportunity for learning.

Dweck's work illustrates that challenges and achievements should be seen as milestones that fuel further development, rather than the end of the road. In a growth mindset, success is not a final destination, but a platform for further growth, leading individuals to stay motivated and push beyond their current limits. This mindset helps maintain a continuous learning loop, where each success drives the pursuit of new goals.

In practice, adopting a growth mindset means seeking feedback, welcoming challenges, and viewing setbacks as part of the growth process. For example, rather than resting on one's laurels after achieving a major career milestone, a person with a growth mindset would reflect on the experience, identify areas for improvement, and set new goals to strive toward. This forward-looking approach creates a sense of dynamism and prevents complacency, ensuring that progress is sustained over time.

Ultimately, Dweck's research reveals that the journey of success is ongoing, and embracing challenges as opportunities for learning helps maintain the drive for continuous improvement. This mindset fosters resilience, adaptability, and long-term fulfilment in personal and professional endeavours.

Embrace Failure: Understand Failure as a Path to Growth

Failure is often seen as a setback, but in reality, it's a springboard for growth. Embracing failure isn't about dwelling on mistakes - it's about leveraging them to fuel success. As Carol Dweck's research on the "growth mindset" (2006) shows, those who view failure as a learning opportunity are more likely to achieve long-term success.

Take Thomas Edison as an example. Before inventing the light bulb, he famously failed 1,000 times. Instead of seeing each attempt as a loss, he viewed each failure as a discovery of what didn't work, inching closer to what would. By embracing failure, Edison turned what could have been discouraging defeats into lessons that ultimately shaped one of the most important inventions of modern times.

When you experience failure, it's essential to reflect and analyze what went wrong. This doesn't mean beating yourself up over mistakes, but rather identifying weak spots in your approach. By dissecting your failure, you uncover valuable insights that can prevent the same mistakes in the future. For example, if a product launch flopped, reviewing the campaign could reveal flaws in the market strategy or a mismatch between customer needs and the product.

Seek Discomfort: Growth Through Challenge

Stepping out of your comfort zone is a powerful way to foster growth. The comfort zone is where routine and familiarity reign, but it's also where complacency can set in. By deliberately seeking discomfort, you push your limits, break free from stagnation, and become more adaptable.

First, reflect on the areas in your life where things feel too easy or routine this is where growth opportunities often lie dormant. For example, if you've become too comfortable in your current role at work, it might be time to take on more responsibilities, such as leading a new project or learning a new technology. When you identify these comfort zones, you can challenge yourself to actively move beyond them.

The next step is to seek out challenges that require you to develop new skills or adopt fresh perspectives. Taking on a project outside your usual scope forces you to stretch yourself and build resilience. For instance, if you're a marketing professional, try exploring data analytics or project management, skills that complement your expertise but take you beyond your current comfort zone. Similarly, if you're used to being an individual contributor, consider stepping up to a leadership role.

Continually engaging in uncomfortable activities builds resilience and adaptability over time. Whether it's public speaking, learning a new language, or networking with unfamiliar people, each experience that pushes your limits will help you grow. The key is consistency—by regularly facing discomfort, you begin to adapt and thrive in new situations.

By actively seeking discomfort, you build resilience and adaptability that will serve you in both personal and professional environment. Embracing challenges opens the door to new opportunities and keeps you moving forward.

Celebrate Milestones, But Don't Linger

Celebrating achievements is important, but staying in that moment for too long can cause you to lose momentum. For example, imagine a student who aces an exam and spends weeks celebrating instead of preparing for the next one. They risk falling behind. It's fine to enjoy your success, but quickly shifting focus to the next goal keeps you moving forward. This could be as simple as celebrating with a dinner and then brainstorming your next steps the following day. Athletes, like marathon runners, often use this approach: after completing a race, they celebrate briefly, then set their sights on improving their time for the next race. This habit of setting new challenges right after celebrating success helps prevent complacency and ensures continued growth.

Take the example of Olympic athletes. These high performers compete on the global stage every four years, representing the pinnacle of athletic achievement. After winning medals and basking in the glory of their accomplishments, they don't take extended breaks. Instead, many athletes begin preparing for the next Olympic cycle almost immediately after their victory.

The Olympics require a mindset of relentless forward progress. Athletes like Michael Phelps and Simone Biles, after achieving incredible feats, always looked ahead to their next challenge. Phelps, after winning his record number of gold medals, famously stated that despite the celebrations, he would always set new goals and push his boundaries even further. Biles, too, after dominating gymnastics, constantly sought to improve her routines for the next competition.

Why do they do this? The Olympic world is ever-evolving—new techniques, training methods, and competitors emerge constantly. Athletes know that if they rest too long on their past victories, they risk losing their competitive edge. The constant pursuit of excellence, fuelled by short but meaningful celebrations, keeps them at the top of their game.

This strategy is not just limited to elite athletes. Marathon runners, for example, often enjoy their accomplishments after crossing the finish line, but within days, many start planning their next race, analyzing their performance, and looking for ways to improve. This constant setting of new goals ensures that they don't fall into a rut, lose their fitness, or stagnate in their training.

In a broader context, professionals, students, and creatives can all learn from this approach. Imagine a student who celebrates a top score on an exam. If they revel in that success for too long without preparing for the next challenge, they risk losing momentum and falling behind academically. The key is to celebrate success, but not let it define the end of the journey. As soon as the celebration ends, it's important to shift focus to the next goal.

Embrace Continuous Learning and Skill Development

Success can sometimes create a false sense of security, where individuals feel they've "arrived" and no longer need to push themselves. However, research shows that continuous learning is crucial for long-term success. **Ericsson et al. (1993)** emphasize the significance of "deliberate practice"—the idea that consistently working to improve specific skills is essential to maintaining and enhancing performance. For instance, a professional who stops learning new skills in a rapidly changing industry risks becoming obsolete. Think of the tech industry, where professionals need to stay up-to-date with the latest software or programming languages to remain competitive.

Investing in professional development, like attending courses or earning new certifications, helps ensure you're not left behind. For example, a manager might pursue a leadership certification to improve team dynamics, while encouraging team members to take online courses can promote a culture of growth. Regularly sharing these new learnings with colleagues fosters collaboration and innovation. Staying on top of industry trends and technological advancements also helps keep a competitive edge. By continuously learning and applying new knowledge, you ensure that success isn't a one-time event but an ongoing journey.

Surround Yourself with Growth-Oriented People

The company you keep plays a vital role in shaping your mindset, behaviours, and ultimately, your success. Surrounding yourself with individuals who are driven, ambitious, and growth-oriented can significantly elevate your own aspirations and keep you motivated.

You are the average of the five people you spend the most time with.

-Jim Rohn, Entrepreneur

Rohn (2007) in his book *"Rising to the top"* encapsulates the idea that your closest relationships can either propel you toward success or keep you stagnant. If you surround yourself with people who challenge you to think bigger and reach higher, you're more likely to adopt their positive habits and embrace a growth mindset.

In a classroom, a dull student who struggles academically may feel demotivated or stuck when surrounded by peers who have similar challenges. However, if this student starts spending time with higher-performing peers, their environment shifts. The bright students often exhibit habits like discipline, curiosity, and resilience. By observing and interacting with these peers, the dull student is more likely to adopt better study habits, seek out challenging problems, and aspire to greater achievements.

The key here is that the dull student isn't inherently less capable but is often limited by their immediate environment. When exposed to bright students who constantly push their boundaries and set higher goals, the dull student begins to internalize these attitudes, thereby shifting from complacency to growth. The reverse is also true: if bright students surround themselves with individuals who don't challenge them or promote complacency, they risk becoming stagnant themselves.

This mirrors the concept **Rohn (2007)** emphasizes—that the people you spend the most time with influence your mindset and actions, which in turn, shape your long-term success or stagnation. Thus, choosing relationships wisely can elevate a person's potential or trap them in mediocrity.

Building meaningful relationships with mentors, peers, and colleagues who prioritize personal development can be a game-changer. For instance, having a mentor in your field who continuously seeks out new knowledge and shares that with you can inspire you to aim for new heights. Engaging in networking opportunities can also help expand your circle of influence. By attending industry events or joining professional organizations, you can meet individuals who share your goals and push you to think outside the box.

Additionally, creating or joining communities that foster continuous learning can provide ongoing support and encouragement. This could be anything from mastermind groups to online forums where members share insights, resources, and motivation to keep pushing forward. Ultimately, aligning yourself with those who inspire you can fuel your own growth, helping you stay on track and maintain a forward-focused mindset.

Set Incremental and Stretch Goals

Setting both incremental and stretch goals can work wonders for maintaining momentum while pushing your limits. Incremental goals serve as stepping stones, helping you to chip away at larger objectives without feeling overwhelmed. For example, if you're training for a marathon, you might start with a goal to run 5 kilometers, then 10 kilometers, and gradually build up to the full distance. Each small win keeps you moving in the right direction, and hitting these milestones gives you a sense of accomplishment that fuels further progress.

Stretch goals, on the other hand, push the envelope and challenge your current capabilities. They make you reach for something just out of your comfort zone, helping you to grow and innovate. Think of a company that has consistently hit its revenue targets—setting a stretch goal to double its annual growth might seem ambitious, but it pushes the team to come up with fresh ideas and strategies.

Locke and Latham's goal-setting theory emphasizes the power of specific, measurable, attainable, relevant, and time-bound (SMART) goals to boost motivation and performance. Their research shows that clearly defined goals—especially ones that stretch your abilities—stimulate focus and effort. When goals are specific, they give you a clear roadmap, and when they're challenging, they push you to perform at higher levels.

To illustrate this, consider a professional setting: if your initial goal is to complete a project, achieving that milestone might tempt you to relax or assume you've done enough. However, if you use this accomplishment as a springboard, you can keep progressing by setting stretch goals—goals that push your limits but are still achievable. For example, after successfully completing a project, your next objective might be to lead a similar project or even spearhead a new initiative that introduces a higher level of complexity or innovation.

The process of breaking larger goals into manageable parts keeps you engaged. When the smaller steps are achieved, it helps you build momentum, giving you the motivation to tackle the next challenge. A key component of Locke and Latham's theory is goal feedback—frequently revisiting and adjusting your goals to fit evolving visions. This allows for continual personal and professional growth, preventing complacency.

This dynamic of constantly raising the bar is especially critical for avoiding the trap of resting on past achievements. Athletes, for instance, use a similar method: after reaching a significant milestone, like winning a championship, they celebrate briefly before setting new targets. Olympians who win gold medals often begin preparing for the next

Olympics shortly after their victory, understanding that success is temporary unless they continue to work toward future accomplishments.

By maintaining this ongoing cycle of review and improvement, you prevent stagnation and stay on the path of growth and learning. Ericsson's deliberate practice model also supports this approach, emphasizing that sustained improvement requires consistently increasing the challenge, even after reaching initial success. This means not settling for past victories but continuing to adjust, stretch, and redefine your goals to match your evolving aspirations.

In sum, specific and challenging goals keep you from *resting on your laurels* and help ensure that your journey of progress is perpetual.

Cultivate a Mindset of Innovation

Cultivating a mindset of innovation is essential to personal growth and preventing complacency after success. Once you've achieved something significant, it's easy to rely on those accomplishments, but true growth requires constant reinvention and exploration. Rather than just refining what you already know, it's important to challenge yourself with new goals and areas for improvement.

For example, you can nurture creativity by setting aside time for passion projects. Whether it's learning a new skill, starting a side hobby, or pursuing something outside your comfort zone, these activities often lead to new insights and can open doors to future opportunities. Much like how taking up a new instrument or sport pushes your mind and body in new directions, this process can lead to personal breakthroughs.

Investing in self-improvement is another critical part of staying innovative. Whether through reading, taking courses, or even engaging in stimulating conversations, the commitment to learning something new helps you keep evolving. Just as artists experiment with new techniques or athletes refine their training methods, consistently updating your knowledge and skills ensures that you stay ahead in your personal development.

Additionally, surrounding yourself with diverse individuals helps bring fresh perspectives into your life. Collaborating or simply engaging in discussions with people from different backgrounds can lead to creative solutions or new ways of thinking that you wouldn't have arrived at on your own. This cross-pollination of ideas is essential for continuous personal growth.

Ultimately, the key to staying innovative and avoiding stagnation is curiosity and the willingness to take risks. By exploring new avenues, investing in personal development, and learning from others, you keep yourself adaptable and open to new possibilities, ensuring ongoing success in both your personal and professional life.

Maintain a Forward-Looking Vision

Staying focused on a forward-looking vision is the secret to avoiding the trap of complacency. It's not just about having a plan; it's about crafting an ambitious dream that constantly pushes you to be better. As **Collins and Porras (1994)** pointed out in their book *"Built to Last"*, having a "Big Hairy Audacious Goal" (BHAG) can feel like aiming for the stars, but that's the point - it pulls you forward, igniting a fire in you that keeps the momentum going.

Imagine it like a lighthouse in a storm—it's not just about navigating the immediate waves, but about keeping your eyes on that bright, distant goal guiding you through the fog of everyday distractions. You need that bold vision to keep pushing the boundaries of what you think is possible. If your goals aren't exciting or a little bit scary, they're probably not pushing you hard enough.

The vision that thrilled you five years ago might feel stale today, and that's okay. Revisiting and tweaking your vision ensures it doesn't become an outdated relic of your past self but a living, breathing roadmap for the future. This adaptability keeps your motivation fresh and relevant.

Consistency is key, too. It's like a mantra—keep reminding yourself of that bigger goal every day. If you align your daily actions with that larger vision, you're not just grinding through tasks; you're making every step count toward that bigger dream. It's like every workout leading up to a marathon—each run, no matter how small, is building you toward the finish line. Without that overarching goal, the small steps can feel pointless, but with it, they gain meaning.

The key challenge, though, is keeping the vision dynamic and relevant. It's easy to become attached to a goal that's no longer serving you, or worse, to achieve it and then feel aimless. That's why it's crucial to keep setting new BHAGs and never let yourself get too comfortable. Once you reach the peak, look for the next mountain to climb.

So, set audacious goals and let them be your guide but don't forget to revisit them, keep them flexible, and make sure every step you take today is aligned with that bold, exciting future you're building for yourself. Keep the fire burning, and never settle!

Surround Yourself with Diverse Perspectives

Surrounding yourself with diverse perspectives is essential to avoiding the trap of complacency after success. As **Page (2009)** emphasizes, diversity in thought is not just a nice-to-have; it's a game-changer for problem-solving and decision-making. When you mix with people who think differently, you're opening the door to new ideas, fresh approaches, and innovative solutions.

Think about it: when you spend time with individuals who challenge you, who see the world through a different lens, it's like injecting a jolt of energy into your mindset. Remember iron sharpens iron. When you're surrounded by driven, ambitious people, their energy is contagious. You start to absorb their habits, their attitudes, and their relentless pursuit of excellence.

Great Mind Discuss Ideas

Average Mind Discuss Events

Small Mind Discuss People

-Eleanor Roosevelt, Diplomat and Activist

Imagine being in a room with a group of dynamic thinkers—each one bringing unique insights and experiences to the table. You might have a brilliant entrepreneur, an artist with a radically different approach, a scientist with a data-driven perspective, and a humanitarian focused on social impact. Together, they create a melting pot of ideas that spark creativity and fuel innovation. Instead of settling for the status quo, you find yourself pushed to explore uncharted territory and think beyond your usual boundaries.

Engaging with these diverse voices not only boosts your creativity but also reshapes your entire approach to challenges. When you hear fresh perspectives on issues you face, it can shift your thinking from "this is how we've always done it" to "what if we tried this instead?" This transformation is crucial, as it keeps complacency at bay and encourages you to continually evolve.

Diversity isn't just about cultural differences; it includes varying experiences, backgrounds, and fields of expertise. The broader the range of perspectives you incorporate into your life, the more well-rounded your understanding of the world becomes. This expanded worldview equips you to tackle problems more effectively and positions you to seize opportunities you might otherwise overlook.

In a rapidly changing world, embracing diverse perspectives isn't just beneficial—it's vital for growth. Surround yourself with those who inspire and challenge you, and watch how it propels you forward. Remember, the journey to greatness isn't a solo endeavour; it's a collaborative effort fuelled by the vibrant ideas and insights of others. So go ahead, seek out those diverse voices, and let their influence sharpen your edge!

Overcoming Mental Blockages

In today's fast-paced world, mental blocks can feel like invisible walls, stopping us in our tracks. Imagine a young entrepreneur with a head full of brilliant ideas, ready to launch a game-changing startup. Just as they're about to leap, a single thought freezes them: *"What if I fail?"* This fear of failure, fueled by the worry of being judged or falling short, locks them in a loop of self-doubt. Instead of chasing their dream, they hold back, letting fear steal opportunities that could change everything.

Now, consider the student who's been working tirelessly on a project, yet every time they sit down to write, a nagging thought creeps in: *"What if it's not perfect?"* Burdened by the weight of perfectionism, they procrastinate, believing only flawless work is acceptable. This relentless pursuit of perfection compromises not only their learning experience but also stifles creativity and growth.

These mental blockages can manifest in various ways. People often say things like *"I'm not good enough"*, *"This won't work,"* *"I can't do this,"* *"I'm not smart enough,"* or *"What if I fail?"*. These phrases reinforce self-doubt and create barriers to success. The inner critic can be relentless, whispering thoughts like *"I'll never measure up"* or *"I'm just not cut out for this"*. Instead of telling ourselves, we can reframe those thoughts to *"I'm learning"* or *"This is an opportunity to grow"*. Recognizing and addressing these limiting beliefs can unlock our true potential.

So, how do we tackle these mental blockages? The key is to shift our mindset from avoiding discomfort to embracing it as a stepping stone for growth. Every successful person has faced their share of challenges and setbacks, and many have learned to turn their failures into valuable lessons.

Remember, success isn't about dodging obstacles; it's about learning to navigate through them. Each setback can become a chance to adapt and emerge stronger. So, let's embrace those bumps in the road, challenge our negative thoughts, and use our experiences as fuel for growth. The only thing standing between you and your dreams might just be those mental barriers. It's time to break them down and step boldly into the future you want!

In the wild, deer are known for their incredible agility and can jump impressive heights—up to 10 feet in the air and distances of over 30 feet. This natural ability is a reflection of their strength, grace, and freedom in their habitat. However, when confined within an enclosure or a small space, a deer may hesitate to jump, even if the height of the barrier is well within its capabilities. This mental blockage arises from a learned behaviour rather than a physical limitation.

This phenomenon can be attributed to the deer's past experiences and conditioning. If a deer is raised in captivity, it may become accustomed to a certain space and develop a fear of jumping beyond its perceived boundaries. This fear can prevent it from tapping into its full potential, illustrating how environmental factors can influence behaviour.

The metaphor extends to human experiences as well. Just like the deer, people often have the potential to achieve great heights but may hold back due to fears, past experiences, or a lack of confidence. It serves as a reminder that breaking free from mental constraints is essential for realizing one's true potential.

Success should be seen as a stepping stone, not a final destination. *Don't Rest on Your Laurels* emphasizes the importance of continuing to strive for excellence even after achieving significant milestones. Embrace failure as a learning opportunity, seek discomfort to foster growth, and surround yourself with people who challenge and inspire you. Continuous learning is essential in a rapidly changing world. The journey to excellence is ongoing, and the best way to honour past achievements is by relentlessly pursuing new goals, avoiding complacency, and maintaining the drive to keep moving forward. Success is a journey, not a conclusion. It is a relentless pursuit of excellence.

EXERCISES

1. Comfort Zone Challenge

Challenge yourself to step outside your comfort zone! Identify **one specific action** you can take this week to shake things up. It could be:

- Starting a conversation with someone new.
- Trying a new hobby or activity that scares you a little.
- Networking with individuals in your field who you admire.

After completing the challenge, take a moment to journal about your experience. How did you feel before and after? What did you learn?

2. Vision Board Creation

Create a **vision board** that visually represents your goals and aspirations beyond your current achievements. Gather images, quotes, and words that inspire you. This board will serve as a daily reminder of your ambitions and the importance of continuous growth.

3. Find Your Accountability Partner

Team up with a friend, colleague, or mentor who shares your drive for growth. Together, set up **regular check-ins** to discuss your progress, share challenges, and celebrate victories. This partnership will keep you motivated and focused on your goals.

4. Goal Setting and Action Plan

It's time to set some powerful goals! Use the **SMART criteria** to define your primary goal:

- **Specific**: What do you want to achieve?
- **Measurable**: How will you measure progress?
- **Achievable**: Is it realistic?
- **Relevant**: How does it align with your values?
- **Time-bound**: What's your deadline?

Outline the steps you need to take, anticipate potential obstacles, and craft a timeline. This blueprint will be your roadmap to success!

5. The "Challenge Yourself" Jar

Create a physical or digital "Challenge Yourself" jar where readers write down actions that push them out of their comfort zone. Encourage them to pull one challenge per week and commit to completing it.

Sample Challenges:

- Speak up in a meeting where you'd usually stay quiet.
- Try learning something new in a field completely outside of your expertise.
- Start a new habit like meditation or journaling.

6. Fear List Exercise

Task: Write down a list of things you're afraid to try and rank them by how intimidating they feel. Choose one from the bottom of the list and commit to trying it this week.

Examples: Present an idea in a meeting, sign up for a fitness class, or share your opinion on a public platform.

Ready, Set, Go!

Completing these exercises will help you recognize the importance of ongoing growth and encourage you to take concrete steps toward your aspirations. Remember, the journey of self-improvement is a marathon, not a sprint. Embrace the process, celebrate your progress, and never forget to keep pushing forward!

Chapter 2: Scope for Improvement: Identifying Growth Opportunities

2.1. Life Long Learning – Road Map to Infinite Growth

In today's rapidly evolving world, the notion that mastering a single skill can sustain a lifetime career is increasingly outdated. Gone are the days when acquiring one skill guaranteed a secure livelihood for life. Each wave of technological advancement reshapes industries, creating new opportunities while rendering old skills obsolete. Lifelong learning has become essential to navigating these changes and securing ongoing success. The rise of digital marketing over the past decade has completely changed how businesses approach advertising. A traditional marketer who focused solely on print or TV ads might have thrived in the early 2000s, but today, they would need to learn digital marketing strategies, including SEO, social media, and data analytics, to stay competitive.

An investment in the knowledge pays best interest.

– Benjamin Franklin, American polymath

The relentless march of technology continuously reshapes the job market. A perfect example is the rise of artificial intelligence (AI). Once, a career as a skilled tradesperson or technician could ensure long-term employment. However, the advent of AI has dramatically altered this landscape. AI's ability to perform tasks ranging from data analysis to customer service has led to significant shifts in the job market, creating a demand for new skills while displacing those who haven't adapted.

For instance, consider the evolution of coding skills. In the early days of computing, knowledge of basic programming languages was sufficient for many roles. However, as AI technologies advance, the complexity of coding has increased, and new programming paradigms have emerged. Skills that were once cutting-edge can quickly become obsolete. A report by the World Economic Forum highlights that over 50% of all employees will need significant reskilling by 2025 due to technological advancements (World Economic Forum, 2020).

The greatest enemy of tomorrow's success is today's success. We have to constantly renew ourselves and adapt to new circumstances.

- Andy Grove, former CEO of Intel.

Consider the story of James Clear, the author of *Atomic Habits*. Before his rise to fame, Clear faced a devastating accident that left him with a broken back. Rather than succumbing to despair, he committed himself to learning everything he could about habit formation and personal development. His rigorous self-study led to profound insights, eventually culminating in a bestselling book that has transformed countless lives. Clear's journey exemplifies how continuous learning can turn adversity into an opportunity for monumental growth.

According to **Tom Senninger's Learning Zone Model**, real development happens when you step into the *stretch zone*—just beyond the comfort zone but not so far that you plunge into the *panic zone*. Senninger's theory divides our experiences into three key zones:

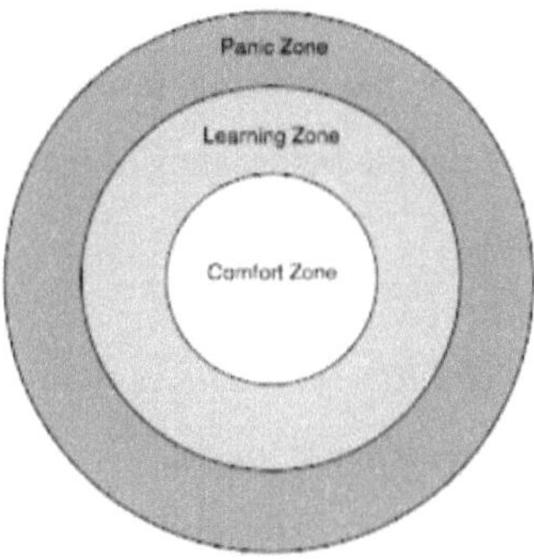

Learning Zone Model

Comfort Zone: This is your "safe space." You feel at ease here, but there's little room for growth. Whether it's a routine job, predictable habits, or tasks you can complete on autopilot, you're not expanding your potential.

Stretch Zone: This is the sweet spot for learning. Here, the challenges are slightly uncomfortable, forcing you to engage more deeply and acquire new skills. It's like exercising a muscle: you need some tension to grow, but too much pressure can cause injury.

Panic Zone: Go too far beyond your capabilities, and you enter the panic zone, where fear and stress can overwhelm you, often causing you to freeze or retreat.

To make this idea more relatable, think of someone with a deep fear of public speaking. In their comfort zone, they avoid speaking engagements altogether, or perhaps only talk to close friends. But growth happens when they stretch—by perhaps joining a small public speaking group, like Toastmasters. The challenges are manageable, and over time, they become more confident. On the flip side, throwing them into a massive arena with thousands of people before they're ready could trigger panic, preventing any progress.

Instead of buying your children all the things you never had, you should teach them all the things you never taught.

-Bruce Lee, Hongkong Martial Artist.

For your own journey, ask yourself: When was the last time you felt truly challenged? Are you still operating within your comfort zone, or have you pushed into that stretch zone recently? And how do you avoid going too far and hitting the panic zone?

This theory isn't just for students or professionals—it applies to anyone eager to push past mental and emotional barriers to achieve personal and professional growth. Whether you're learning a new skill, building relationships, or tackling a big project, the goal is to stretch, not stress.

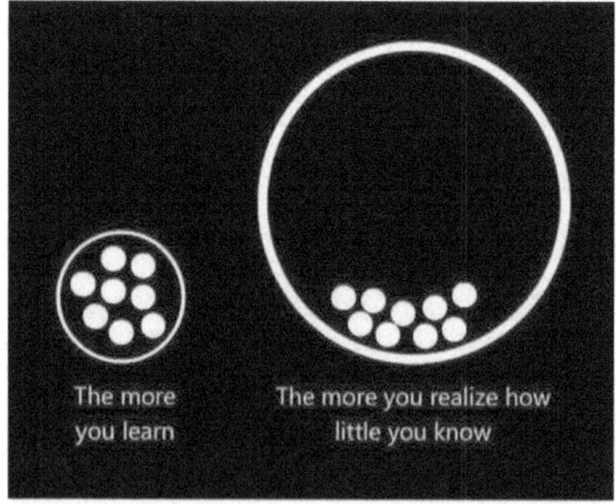

Learning is a fascinating journey. When you start, everything feels new and exciting, and you might think, "I've got this!" But the deeper you go, the more you uncover just how vast the subject is. Suddenly, you realize there's so much more to explore, and what you thought was the whole picture is just a small piece of a much bigger puzzle. This isn't a sign that you're falling behind—it's proof that you're growing. The more you learn, the more curious and open you become, because you understand that true mastery is about staying a student forever. It's easy to fall into the trap of thinking, "I've achieved enough," and stop pushing yourself. But resting on your laurels is like pausing halfway up a mountain—if you stop climbing, you'll never see the breath-taking views waiting at the top.

When you embrace the idea that there's always more to know, life becomes exciting again. Every day becomes an opportunity to grow, discover, and improve. So, don't let the comfort of what you've already achieved hold you back. Stay curious, stay hungry, and remember—the greatest part of your journey is still ahead.

Jack Mezirow's Transformative Learning Theory (1991) emphasizes that critical reflection can lead to profound shifts in a person's worldview. A compelling illustration of this can be found in the life of Nelson Mandela. After spending 27 years in prison for his activism against apartheid, Mandela emerged not with bitterness, but with a renewed commitment to reconciliation and justice. During his time in prison, Mandela reflected deeply on the nature of freedom, leadership, and forgiveness. This reflection led to his transformation from an anti-apartheid activist into a global symbol of peace and unity. His ability to learn, adapt, and transform his perspectives based on his experiences embodies the essence of Mezirow's theory.

Carol Dweck's Growth Mindset Theory (2006) further underscores the importance of a learning-oriented attitude. Dweck's research reveals that individuals with a growth mindset believe that abilities and intelligence can be developed through effort. This mindset is vividly illustrated by the career of comedian Tina Fey. Early in her career, Fey faced numerous challenges, including being overlooked for roles and experiencing creative setbacks. Instead of being discouraged, she leaned into these difficulties as opportunities for growth, consistently honing her skills as a writer, performer, and producer.

A perfect example of her growth mindset is her approach to "Saturday Night Live" (SNL), where she initially worked as a writer. Despite the high-pressure environment and the steep learning curve, Fey didn't see obstacles as insurmountable; she saw them as part of her development. With hard work, she transitioned into one of the head writers of the show and went on to create and star in "30 Rock," a ground-breaking comedy series that garnered widespread acclaim.

Her perseverance, adaptability, and focus on improvement exemplify how the growth mindset operates. Like Dweck's theory suggests, Fey didn't see her abilities as fixed; she viewed setbacks as learning opportunities, which allowed her to rise to the top of her field. Even after achieving immense success, Fey continues to challenge herself with new projects, further reinforcing the idea that growth is an ongoing process. This attitude has not only led to her professional success but has also made her an influential figure in the entertainment industry.

In the age of information, ignorance is a choice. If you are not continually learning, you are falling behind.

- William Pollard, physicist and clergyman.

Gary Becker's Theory of Human Capital (1964) underscores the idea that education and skill development enhance an individual's productivity and economic value. Consider Satya Nadella, CEO of Microsoft, who attributes much of his success to his continuous learning and growth. When Nadella took the reins at Microsoft, he ushered in a cultural shift within the company, moving it from a "know-it-all" to a "learn-it-all" mindset. Nadella encouraged employees to upskill and adapt, fueling Microsoft's transformation into a cloud-first company. His investment in human capital, both personally and organizationally, has paid dividends as Microsoft continues to thrive in the ever-evolving tech landscape.

Another example is the late Steve Jobs, who famously dropped out of college but continued to educate himself in areas that fascinated him, such as calligraphy and design. His relentless curiosity and continuous pursuit of knowledge contributed to the innovation of Apple products. Jobs' belief in cross-disciplinary learning paid off when he designed aesthetically pleasing and user-friendly products that revolutionized the tech world. His success proves that investing in one's human capital, even in unconventional ways, can yield extraordinary outcomes.

As the idiom goes, "you reap what you sow." Both Nadella and Jobs sowed seeds of learning and development that blossomed into ground-breaking achievements, reinforcing Becker's theory that investing in one's human capital is a sure path to success.

Abraham Maslow's concept of self-actualization (1943) emphasizes realizing one's potential and pursuing personal growth. An excellent example of this is Julia Child, whose journey of continuous learning and passion for cooking shaped her extraordinary career. Child didn't start as a chef but learned cooking later in life, constantly expanding her culinary knowledge and skills. Her curiosity for different techniques and cultures led to ground-breaking contributions to French cuisine and inspired millions of home cooks. Walt Disney said, "Keep moving forward", a phrase that speaks to the essence of continuous learning and the pursuit of dreams, much like Child's relentless quest for culinary mastery.

2.2. Setting New Goals after achieving success

Achieving success is a great accomplishment, but it's not the end of the road—it's the starting point for something new. Once you've celebrated, the key is to use those achievements as motivation to set new goals and continue growing. Reflecting on past experiences, as Donald Schön's Theory of Reflective Practice emphasizes the importance of continuously learning from one's experiences, both successes and failures, to improve professional competency and personal growth. At its core, the theory revolves around two key processes: **reflection-in-action** and **reflection-on-action. Reflection-in-Action** occurs during the moment of action, where professionals think on their feet, reassess their decisions, and adapt to the unfolding situation. For example, a teacher might notice that students are disengaged during a lesson and quickly change their approach—perhaps by incorporating a discussion or using examples that resonate better with the class. By actively thinking and adjusting mid-action, individuals can improve outcomes in real-time.

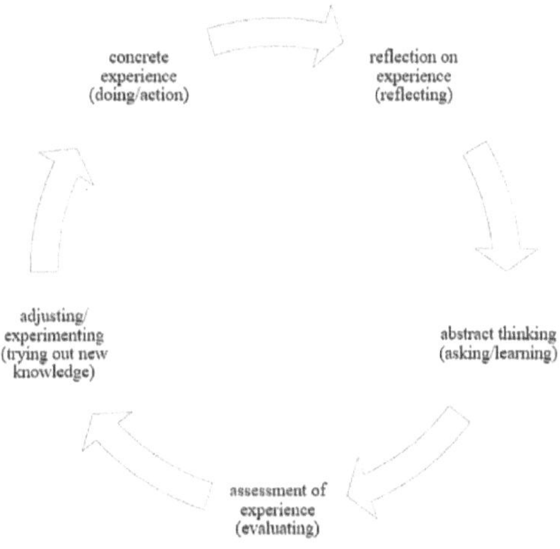

**Theory of "reflection-in-action"
and "reflection-on-action"**

Reflection-on-Action happens after the event, where individuals review and analyze their actions, outcomes, and decisions to extract valuable lessons. For instance, after completing a project, a team might gather to discuss what went well and what didn't, identifying areas for improvement. This post-mortem process allows for thoughtful learning and prepares them to tackle future challenges more effectively. Schön's theory suggests that by engaging in these reflective practices, individuals can build a repertoire of knowledge that combines theoretical understanding with real-world experience. This iterative process of reflection and application fosters innovation, adaptability, and deeper professional expertise.

For example, a healthcare professional dealing with a challenging patient might reflect on their interaction, recognize missed cues, and explore how a different approach could have led to better outcomes. The insights gained can then inform future practices, ensuring continuous improvement.

Steve Jobs after founding Apple and facing both success and failure, he didn't let early achievements or setbacks define him. Instead, Jobs used his past experiences to fuel his return to Apple in 1997, leading to ground-breaking innovations like the iPhone and iPad. He took the time to reflect, learn, and push beyond past successes.

Another great example is Oprah Winfrey. After achieving massive success as a talk show host, Oprah didn't stop there. She continuously reflected on her work and found new ways to make an impact, launching her own network, producing films, and becoming a powerful voice in various social causes. This shows how reflecting on achievements, learning from them, and then setting new goals keeps the journey exciting and impactful.

Setting new goals becomes more effective when you apply the **SMART criteria**—goals that are **Specific**, **Measurable**, **Achievable**, **Relevant**, and **Time-bound**. A great example of this approach is Taylor Swift's strategic reinvention with her album *1989*. After achieving massive success, including multiple Grammy Awards, Swift didn't settle. She set a SMART goal to shift her musical style from country to pop, aiming to reach specific commercial milestones within a set timeframe. Her clear, actionable goals included creating a new sound and expanding her fan base, and they helped her achieve further commercial and critical success. This showcases how SMART goals can turn vision into reality.

Balancing long-term and short-term goals is another crucial factor for sustained success. **Edwin Locke and Gary Latham's Goal Setting**

Theory emphasizes the need for a combination of overarching objectives and practical short-term steps to stay on track. Jeff Bezos's approach with Amazon and Blue Origin exemplifies this strategy. Bezos set a grand vision of making space exploration more accessible and eventually colonizing space. To support this long-term goal, he focused on short-term objectives like developing the New Shepard rocket for suborbital spaceflight. By aligning ambitious dreams with concrete, actionable steps, Bezos was able to drive progress in both Amazon's growth and his space exploration venture.

Staying motivated and holding yourself accountable are the fuel that drives long-term success. **Deci and Ryan's Self-Determination Theory (2004)** suggests that motivation flourishes when you feel autonomous, competent, and connected to others. Oprah Winfrey is a perfect example of this. Throughout her career, she has remained highly motivated by setting her own goals, continuously challenging herself, and staying deeply connected to her audience. By sharing her personal growth journey, struggles, and triumphs publicly, Oprah has held herself accountable in a way that inspires millions. Her willingness to be vulnerable about her experiences, whether it's about health, career, or emotional well-being, keeps her motivated and in tune with her purpose.

One clear instance of Oprah's commitment to this principle is her work with the Oprah Book Club. Not only does she set goals for herself to keep learning and evolving through reading, but she also engages her community in the process, keeping herself accountable by sharing her reflections with millions. This combination of autonomy, mastery, and connection embodies Deci and Ryan's theory, showing how these factors keep motivation high.

Similarly, Michael Jordan's drive exemplifies how motivation can thrive under accountability. Known for setting incredibly high standards, Jordan pushed himself to new heights by constantly measuring his progress, seeking feedback, and maintaining a competitive edge. His rigorous work ethic and mindset towards always improving made him one of the greatest athletes of all time. His famous quote, "I've failed over and over and over again in my life. And that is why I succeed," demonstrates how self-accountability and motivation go hand in hand.

Whether you're building a media empire like Oprah or dominating the basketball court like Jordan, the lesson is clear: staying motivated requires not only setting goals but also creating systems of accountability that challenge and inspire growth. Motivation isn't a one-time boost; it's a steady flame, kept alive by self-determination, accountability, and a connection to your larger purpose.

2.3. The Role of Innovation: Staying Ahead by Constantly Innovating

Innovation is like the heartbeat of progress. In our fast-moving world, where technology and trends change almost daily, staying ahead means constantly coming up with new ideas and improving on them. This chapter dives into why innovation is so important, using easy-to-understand theories, real-life examples, and inspiring quotes from some of the most successful people in history.

Understanding Innovation: Why It Matters

Innovation is what drives the world forward. It's the spark that turns ideas into reality and transforms everyday life. It's not just about big, flashy inventions—it's about seeing things differently and finding better ways to solve problems. Innovation means challenging the way things are and imagining how they could be. It's that moment of creativity where something new is born, something that changes the game.

At the heart of every great achievement is someone who dared to think outside the box, who didn't settle for "good enough." True innovators keep pushing forward, even when things get tough. They see failure as part of the journey, not the end. The world's most creative minds know that it's not just about having ideas; it's about turning those ideas into action.

In today's fast-moving world, standing still isn't an option. To lead, you have to be willing to take risks, try new things, and break the mold. That's how innovation happens—and that's how you get ahead. Why follow when you can lead? Innovation is the key to staying on top, and those who embrace it are the ones who shape the future. As Steve Jobs said, *"Innovation distinguishes between a leader and a follower,"* highlighting the critical role innovation plays in setting leaders apart from the crowd.

Everett Rogers' Diffusion of Innovations Theory (1962) demonstrates that innovation spreads in stages, starting with "innovators" who are the first to adopt new ideas. Historical examples provide us with some fascinating insights into how individuals drove innovation and changed society.

One great example from the past is Thomas Edison, whose relentless curiosity and drive led to the invention of the lightbulb, phonograph, and many other ground-breaking innovations. Edison didn't just wait for change to happen—he created it. His approach wasn't just about invention, but about mass-producing and commercializing technology in ways that would revolutionize daily life for millions of people. Edison embodies the spirit of innovation, shaping industries that didn't exist before.

Another fascinating figure is Marie Curie, the pioneering physicist and chemist who discovered radium and polonium. Despite immense obstacles, including gender discrimination, she pushed the boundaries of scientific knowledge, winning two Nobel Prizes. Her innovative research in radioactivity not only transformed the field of chemistry but also opened doors to ground-breaking medical treatments, changing the course of history.

Nikola Tesla is yet another innovator who fits Rogers' model. Though not always recognized during his lifetime, Tesla's visionary ideas on alternating current (AC) power transformed how electricity was delivered. His ground-breaking work laid the foundation for modern electrical systems, driving innovation in energy distribution and opening new possibilities for global development.

These examples from history show that the impact of innovation is not limited to a particular era. Individuals like Edison, Curie, and Tesla each took bold risks, creating entirely new fields and influencing generations to come. Their legacies continue to shape the way we live today.

Innovation can also be as simple as rethinking the small things. Take James Dyson, for example. While vacuum cleaners existed for decades, James Dyson reinvented the product with bagless technology, transforming how people cleaned their homes. His innovation wasn't creating something entirely new but taking an existing product and making it better.

In both personal and professional spheres, innovation is the tool that pushes boundaries, breaks limitations, and opens new doors. Whether it's the pioneering work of Marie Curie in radioactivity or Thomas Edison's relentless drive to invent and commercialize groundbreaking technologies like the lightbulb, the power of innovation is undeniable. To stay competitive, individuals and organizations need to foster a mindset that is always searching for the next great idea—just like Nikola Tesla, whose visionary ideas on alternating current transformed the world. It's that forward-thinking mentality that sets people apart and propels them into uncharted territory.

Disruptive Innovation: Changing the Game

Disruptive innovations usually start at the bottom of the market, serving a niche group, but with time, they evolve and become so important that they revolutionize how things are done across the board. **Clayton Christensen's Theory of Disruptive Innovation (1997)** provides a groundbreaking framework for understanding how new entrants, often with simpler or more affordable solutions, can revolutionize established industries. At its heart, the theory highlights the dynamics between sustaining innovations, which enhance existing products for established markets, and disruptive innovations, which create new markets or redefine existing ones by prioritizing accessibility, affordability, and simplicity. Targets underserved or entirely new customer segments by offering a more accessible, often lower-cost solution. Over time, these innovations improve and capture the mainstream market. A classic example is the emergence of budget airlines, which initially catered to cost-sensitive travelers but eventually captured a significant portion of the broader market.

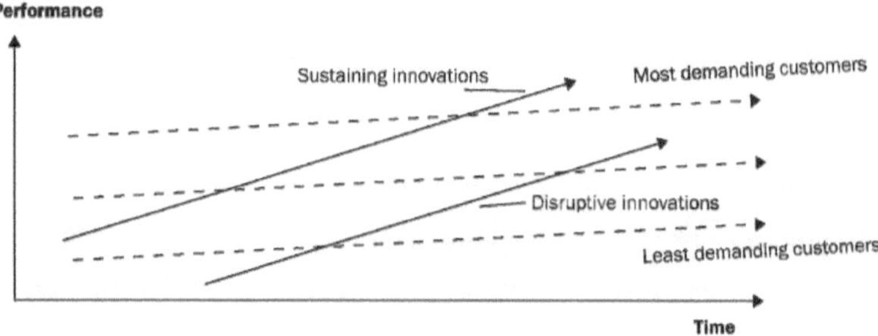

Disruptive Innovation Theory

Another example is of Uber, which started as a ride-sharing service for a small group of users in San Francisco. It didn't compete directly with taxis at first, but by offering a more convenient, cheaper, and tech-driven alternative, Uber has since disrupted the entire transportation industry, forcing traditional taxi services to adapt or be left behind.

The only way to discover the limits of the possible is to go beyond them into the impossible.

- Arthur C. Clarke's, Fiction Writer

This quote directly speaks about the spirit of disruptive innovation. It's about pushing boundaries, trying things that others might dismiss as unfeasible, and in the process, transforming the landscape.

Another compelling example is Airbnb, which began as a way for people to rent out their spare rooms. It started with a small, under-served market—those looking for cheaper alternatives to hotels. Today, it's transformed the hospitality industry, with hotels now having to compete with homeowners across the globe.

In each of these cases, the innovators pushed beyond the possible into what once seemed impossible, turning small ideas into game-changing revolutions. This is the essence of disruptive innovation—challenging norms, shaking up industries, and unlocking new opportunities for growth and progress. It's a reminder that success often comes not from following the well-trodden path but from venturing into the unknown.

Adopting an Innovation Mindset: Always Improving

Carol Dweck's Growth Mindset Theory (2006) is all about believing that our abilities can grow with effort and practice. This mindset is crucial for innovation because it means seeing challenges as opportunities to learn and improve. When you have a growth mindset, you're more likely to keep trying new things, learn from mistakes, and keep moving forward.

Thomas Edison, known for inventing the lightbulb, faced many failures before succeeding. His quote highlights that failure is just a part of the process. It's about trying many different ways until you find what works. This perseverance is key to successful innovation.

I have not failed. I've just found 10,000 ways that won't work .

-Thomas Edison

This quote perfectly captures the essence of a growth mindset. Instead of seeing his unsuccessful attempts as failures, Edison viewed them as necessary steps toward eventual success. His willingness to persist in the face of adversity is what ultimately led to his ground breaking innovations.

Similarly, Dweck's theory explains that when we adopt a growth mindset, we approach challenges with enthusiasm, understanding that with effort, we can always improve. Steve Jobs, for instance, didn't let setbacks like being ousted from Apple in 1985 stop him. Instead, he learned from the experience, started NeXT and Pixar, and later returned to Apple to lead the creation of world-changing products like the iPhone and iPad.

Innovation thrives in environments where challenges are seen as opportunities for growth, and this mindset ensures that perseverance leads to ground-breaking success. In essence, to innovate effectively, one must be willing to fail—because, as Edison and Jobs demonstrated, failures are often the stepping stones to transformative achievements.

Open Innovation: Working Together for Greater Results

Look at **Lev Vygotsky's Sociocultural Theory (1978),** which emphasizes the importance of social interaction in learning and development. According to Vygotsky, knowledge is constructed through social engagement and collaboration with others, rather than in isolation. Vygotsky stressed that learning is inherently social. Interaction with others exposes individuals to new ideas, challenges their thinking, and fosters deeper understanding. He introduced the idea of the Zone of Proximal Development (ZPD), which is the gap between what an individual can achieve independently and what they can accomplish with the guidance of a more knowledgeable other (MKO), such as a teacher, peer, or parent. For example, a child may struggle to solve a math problem alone but can succeed with step-by-step guidance from a teacher. The ZPD highlights the potential for learning through targeted support.

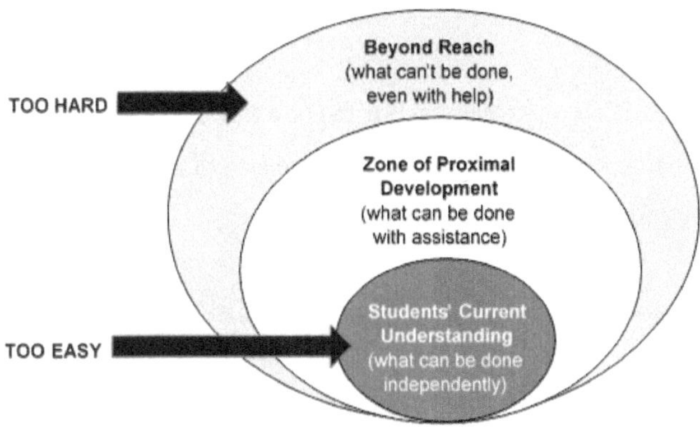

Sociocultural Theory

Relating this to open innovation, Vygotsky's theory highlights how personal growth and success can be significantly amplified when we collaborate and seek out external input. Just like in the ZPD, where a learner achieves more with the help of a mentor or peer, individuals or organizations can innovate more effectively by leveraging ideas and expertise from others. Whether it's through partnerships, mentorships, or knowledge-sharing, collaboration leads to faster learning and more robust solutions than working in isolation.

For instance, if you're trying to develop a new skill or solve a complex problem, working with others who bring different experiences or expertise can help you overcome barriers that might have held you back if you worked alone. This mirrors Vygotsky's concept of learning through social interaction, where you expand your capabilities by tapping into the collective knowledge around you.

Alone we can do so little; together we can do so much

- Helen Keller, American Author

Helen Keller's quote emphasizes the power of working together. In open innovation, combining ideas and resources with others leads to better and faster results than working alone.

The Continuous Innovation Loop: Keep Evolving

Innovation isn't a one-time event—it's an ongoing cycle, a dynamic loop that thrives on adaptability and resilience. The idea behind the **Continuous Innovation Loop** is simple yet powerful: to remain relevant and competitive, individuals, teams, and organizations must embrace an endless process of learning, experimenting, and improving. It's about never settling for "good enough" and constantly asking, *"What's next?"*. **Eric Ries' Lean Startup methodology (2011)** introduces the idea of the Continuous Innovation Loop. This approach involves regularly testing and improving ideas through cycles of building, measuring, and learning. Instead of making a big change all at once, you make small improvements continuously based on feedback. This helps businesses stay adaptable and keep up with changes in the market.

Innovation is the ability to see change as an opportunity—not a threat.
— Steve Jobs, American Businessmen

Steve Jobs's quote here reminds us that innovation isn't just about reacting to change but about seeing it as a chance to grow and improve. Embracing change as an opportunity helps keep ideas fresh and relevant.

Instant Gratification – An enemy to innovation

Instant gratification is the desire for immediate rewards and satisfaction, often at the expense of future benefits. In today's fast-paced world, it's easy to fall into this mindset, thanks to things like social media, instant messaging, and on-demand services. However, this can lead to impatience and poor decision-making, as we prioritize short-term pleasure over long-term success.

Take the Marshmallow Test conducted by psychologist Walter Mischel in the 1960s as an example. Children were offered a marshmallow and given the choice to either eat it immediately or wait and receive two marshmallows later. The study revealed that those who were able to delay gratification tended to have better life outcomes, including higher academic achievement and stronger emotional coping mechanisms later in life.

The growing lust for instant gratification and success in today's generation can be attributed to several cultural, technological, and societal factors. The rise of the internet, smartphones, and social media has made almost everything available at the touch of a button. Whether it's ordering food, streaming movies, or receiving validation through likes and comments, we've become accustomed to instant rewards. This constant availability of quick results has diminished the patience required for long-term efforts. A study by the Royal Society for Public Health found that teenagers very active on social media platforms users reported higher levels of anxiety and depression compared to non-users, highlighting the platform's role in fostering unrealistic expectations and comparisons. A teenager may find it hard to sit through a two-hour study session without interruptions, feeling the constant urge to check their phone for notifications.

Social media platforms are engineered to tap into the brain's reward system, providing a potent cocktail of instant engagement and validation. Every "like," "comment," or "share" triggers a surge of dopamine—a feel-good neurotransmitter—making these platforms incredibly addictive. While this immediate feedback loop offers quick satisfaction, it fosters a culture of instant gratification that can have profound negative impacts, particularly on teenagers. The curated, polished lives showcased on social media create unrealistic standards. Teens may develop a distorted sense of reality, believing that success and happiness are immediate and effortless.

Neuroplasticity of brain

The concept of neuroplasticity demonstrates that the brain can continue evolving even after the age of 60. Traditionally, it was believed that cognitive decline was inevitable with aging, but recent studies have proven otherwise. The brain retains its ability to form new neural pathways through activities like learning, physical exercise, and social engagement. Cognitive reserve, which helps the brain adapt and stay resilient against age-related issues, can be enhanced through continuous mental stimulation, such as learning new skills or hobbies. Research has shown that neurogenesis, the formation of new neurons, still occurs in older adults, particularly in the hippocampus, a region responsible for memory and learning. Regular physical exercise, such as walking or yoga, boosts this process by increasing oxygen flow to the brain. Furthermore, emotional and social involvement plays a significant role in sustaining brain health, fostering connections that encourage cognitive growth. This suggests that lifelong learning and engagement can preserve and even enhance brain functions well into later years, offering a hopeful perspective on aging and cognitive development. It underscores the idea that the brain is adaptable and capable of growth, regardless of age.

2.4. Strategic Growth Framework

This framework encompasses the essential approaches for continuous improvement and development across personal and professional spheres. It highlights the importance of ongoing learning, goal-setting, and innovation as interconnected elements driving sustained progress and success.

Cultivate Curiosity

Cultivating curiosity is a vital component of any strategic growth framework. At its core, curiosity fuels the desire to learn, explore, and question the status quo. When you cultivate curiosity, you create an environment where innovation thrives, and complacency is challenged. This mindset not only keeps you motivated and engaged but also helps you adapt to changing circumstances and discover new opportunities. By regularly questioning existing processes, exploring alternative solutions, and staying informed about industry trends, you ensure that your approach to growth remains dynamic and forward-thinking. Curiosity is the engine that drives continuous improvement and sustained success.

Consider a young child who, upon seeing a bird fly, asks their parent, "Why does the bird fly?" When the parent explains that birds have wings that help them fly, the child might then ask, "Why do birds have wings?" and "Why can't people fly like birds?". Each answer only opens the door to more questions. That snowball effect of curiosity drives their hunger for knowledge.

However, curiosity doesn't have to fade with age—it can evolve into a powerful tool for personal and professional growth in adulthood. The same drive to learn and explore that guided us as children can be harnessed to push boundaries, foster creativity, and open new doors. In adults, curiosity transforms from simple questioning into a strategic mindset, where asking "why" and "what if" becomes essential to navigating complex challenges and discovering innovative solutions.

In the workplace, for example, curiosity is the engine of innovation. When adults continuously question existing processes, they identify inefficiencies, propose improvements, and develop new strategies that can lead to breakthroughs. Curiosity pushes professionals to stay updated with industry trends, research new technologies, and challenge the status quo, leading to career advancement and organizational success.

In relationships, curiosity helps adults deepen connections and enhance communication. Asking thoughtful questions, listening intently, and showing genuine interest in others' perspectives cultivates empathy and strengthens bonds. In personal growth, curiosity encourages lifelong learning, whether through picking up new skills, exploring unfamiliar cultures, or breaking out of comfort zones to gain fresh experiences.

Moreover, adults can leverage curiosity to adapt to change. In a rapidly evolving world, those who remain curious are better equipped to embrace new technologies, pivot in uncertain times, and thrive in dynamic environments. Curiosity keeps the mind agile and resilient, allowing adults to stay relevant and continue evolving.

The beauty of curiosity is that it transcends age—it is not just for the young. As adults, the questions may become more sophisticated, but the underlying desire to understand, grow, and explore remains the same. By nurturing curiosity, adults can transform their outlook on life, turning everyday experiences into opportunities for learning and growth.

Set Learning Goals

Setting learning goals is a powerful way to ensure you're always moving forward. Just like a samurai prepares for battle with intention and focus, you must approach your learning with the same level of precision. By using the **SMART framework**—Specific, Measurable, Achievable, Relevant, and Time-bound—you create a clear path that leads to meaningful progress. These goals act as your compass, guiding you through the maze of distractions and helping you stay on course, step by step.

Take a moment to imagine this: Instead of saying, "I want to learn more about digital marketing," think like a Japanese craftsman, dedicated to perfecting their art. A SMART goal could be, "I will complete a certification course in digital marketing within three months by studying for two hours each day." This is akin to the concept of *kaizen*—the Japanese principle of continuous improvement. By breaking down your learning into specific, manageable tasks, you ensure that progress is made every day, no matter how small.

In Japanese culture, discipline and structure are highly valued, seen in everything from the meticulous care of a bonsai tree to the artistry of tea ceremonies. Applying this mindset to learning means not leaving growth up to chance but instead crafting a plan. For example, if you want to master a new language like Japanese, don't merely aim to "learn Japanese." Set a SMART goal: "I will complete the beginner-level lessons in the Genki textbook in six weeks, dedicating an hour every evening."

This process creates a roadmap—each chapter or lesson becomes a milestone, and every achievement is a moment to celebrate, much like the gradual blooming of a cherry blossom, which signals the arrival of spring.

Just as a skilled martial artist selects the right weapon for their training, choosing the right resources for learning is crucial. Suppose you want to dive deeper into a Japanese skill, like the art of calligraphy (*shodo*). Instead of just wishing to "be good at calligraphy," set a goal: "I will practice three different kanji characters daily using online tutorials and finish one piece each week for three months." This gives you a timeline and allows you to track your progress.

Incorporating specific tools such as online classes, books, podcasts, or learning apps helps you stay grounded. In Japan, the practice of lifelong learning, known as *shugyo*, is revered. Whether it's improving one's craft or acquiring new knowledge, the mindset is to keep evolving.

The Japanese culture teaches us that mastery comes not from leaps but from a series of small, intentional steps. The ritual of setting goals ensures that your learning process mirrors this slow, deliberate progress. Instead of overwhelming yourself with grand ambitions, break them down into smaller goals that you can tackle one by one, much like the art of *origami*, where a simple sheet of paper transforms into intricate beauty through a series of precise folds.

By embracing this approach, you will discover that learning is not a sprint but a marathon—one that requires patience, dedication, and the wisdom to celebrate small victories along the way. So, take inspiration from the Japanese dedication to precision, mindfulness, and continuous growth. Start today by outlining what skills or knowledge you want to acquire and how you plan to achieve them. Equip yourself with the right resources, set timelines, and break down your learning into achievable steps. With a clear roadmap, consistent effort, and a touch of patience, you'll not only achieve your learning goals but also embody the spirit of lifelong learning.

Embrace Challenges

Embracing challenges is crucial for growth and development. Recognize that setbacks and difficulties are not obstacles but integral components of the learning journey. When faced with challenges, instead of being discouraged, view them as opportunities to gain insights and improve. Analyze mistakes thoroughly to understand what went wrong and why, and use this understanding to make informed adjustments and enhancements. By adopting this mindset, you turn failures into stepping stones for success, fostering resilience and continuous improvement. This approach not only enhances your problem-solving skills but also encourages a proactive attitude toward overcoming future obstacles. A prime example of this attitude is Sylvester Stallone's journey. Before becoming a Hollywood legend, Stallone faced crushing rejections and financial hardship. His script for "Rocky" was turned down over and over, and he struggled to make ends meet as a small-time actor. Many would have thrown in the towel, but Stallone did the opposite. He kept pushing, believing in his vision, and refusing to compromise. When he finally sold the script, he accepted a low payment but insisted on playing the lead role. His persistence paid off when "Rocky" became a box-office hit, earning multiple Academy Awards and launching his career.

Stallone's story is a reminder that embracing challenges can lead to breakthroughs. Had he given up after his initial failures, he would never have experienced the triumph that followed. His perseverance turned adversity into an opportunity for greatness. Stallone didn't just overcome the odds—he used them to fuel his success.

This kind of determination is what makes embracing challenges so important. Every challenge you face is a chance to become better. Whether it's learning a new skill, tackling a tough project at work, or pushing yourself in your personal life, stepping outside your comfort zone forces you to grow. By constantly stretching your abilities, you build resilience and develop new ways of thinking.

Instead of avoiding difficult situations, dive headfirst into them. Approach each one as a chance to improve and move forward. Even if you stumble along the way, take time to analyze your mistakes and figure out what went wrong. Understanding your missteps not only helps you adjust your approach but also makes you more prepared for future obstacles. Failure isn't the end—it's a chance to pivot and keep going with more knowledge and insight.

In the end, challenges are what make success feel truly rewarding. Every setback teaches you something new, strengthens your character, and brings you one step closer to your goals. So, embrace the tough moments, knowing they are just part of the process. Great things never come from comfort zones, and by facing challenges head-on, you can transform your failures into stepping stones for long-term success.

Next time you're faced with a difficult task, think of it as your personal "Rocky moment." Push through, learn from the experience, and keep moving forward. Every challenge is a chance to become a better, stronger version of yourself, and the rewards will be well worth the effort. Embrace challenges, and let them fuel your path to greatness!

Utilize Diverse Learning Resources

Utilizing diverse learning resources such as online courses, webinars, and educational apps can significantly enhance your educational experience by offering flexibility and access to a broad range of knowledge and skills. Online courses, which are structured programs delivered over the internet, provide the flexibility to learn at your own pace and on your own schedule. This adaptability allows you to balance other responsibilities while exploring a wide array of subjects and specializations. Many online courses also offer certificates upon completion, which can be valuable for career advancement.

Kim Kardashian provides a compelling example of returning to school and achieving notable success. In 2018, Kardashian enrolled in a criminal justice reform program at the University of California, Los Angeles (UCLA) to deepen her understanding of the legal system and enhance her efforts in criminal justice reform. This decision followed her high-profile advocacy work, including lobbying for the release of incarcerated individuals and championing various criminal justice reform initiatives.

Kardashian's commitment to education in this field significantly amplified her influence and effectiveness in her advocacy work. By returning to school and immersing herself in legal studies, she was able to contribute more meaningfully to discussions and reforms surrounding criminal justice. Her educational pursuits not only bolstered her credibility but also exemplified how public figures can leverage education to drive positive change in societal issues. Her journey highlights a valuable lesson: education is a lifelong pursuit, and it's never too late to return to school, attend a webinar, or download an educational app to refine your skills. The knowledge you gain, combined with your passion and experience, can set you apart and open new doors—whether it's for career advancement or personal fulfillment.

Build a Supportive Network

Building a supportive network is like planting a tree—it takes time, care, and the right environment to grow. Surrounding yourself with people who value learning creates a space where ideas flow, motivation soars, and success becomes a shared goal. Your network isn't just a group of people; it's your powerhouse for growth, providing encouragement, fresh insights, and new perspectives that challenge your assumptions.

Imagine regular discussions with like-minded peers, mentors, and even students. These interactions keep you on your toes, pushing you to stay updated and think outside the box. It's not just about learning for yourself—sharing your insights and experiences helps others grow too, creating a cycle of mutual empowerment. In this way, everyone in the network benefits, and together, you create a culture of continuous improvement.

Take inspiration from India's own tech entrepreneur, N. R. Narayana Murthy, co-founder of Infosys. Murthy built a solid support network that included not just his business partners, but also mentors who guided him and peers who believed in his vision. He surrounded himself with talented individuals who challenged him, learned from him, and contributed to Infosys becoming a global IT powerhouse. His supportive network allowed him to navigate challenges, stay ahead of industry trends, and continuously innovate.

You can also look at India's educational leader Dr. APJ Abdul Kalam, the "Missile Man of India." His journey was marked by strong mentorship from his teachers and peers. Kalam was known for his lifelong learning approach and building teams where every member contributed to scientific advancements. His story reminds us that building a supportive network is about more than personal gain—it's about uplifting others while propelling yourself forward.

So, how can you build your own circle of growth? Start by finding mentors who can offer guidance, feedback, and advice based on their knowledge and experience. Mentors are like lighthouses in your journey—they don't steer your ship but help you navigate through challenges and uncertainties. Peer networks can be equally valuable, offering collaboration, fresh insights, and mutual motivation.

Reflect and Adapt

In the journey of personal and professional development, **reflecting and adapting** are like your compass and map—they keep you on track and help you navigate the unexpected. Taking time to reflect on your actions, progress, and setbacks gives you valuable insights into what's working and where improvements are needed. This is the moment when you pause, look back at your journey, and recognize your strengths, while also being honest about the areas that require more attention.

When you reflect, you begin to spot patterns in your decisions, habits, and outcomes. This self-awareness is a powerful tool that helps you refine your approach moving forward. Imagine if, after every project, every meeting, or every task, you took a moment to ask, *What did I learn from this?* This simple act of reflection can uncover golden insights that will shape how you tackle future challenges.

A great example of a tennis player who exemplifies the power of reflection and adaptation is Rafael Nadal. Known for his resilience and strong work ethic, Nadal constantly assesses his performance, both during and after matches, to learn and improve. Early in his career, he relied heavily on his forehand and agility, which made him nearly unbeatable on clay courts but sometimes vulnerable on faster surfaces. Recognizing this, Nadal adapted by working on his serve, backhand, and net game, which eventually allowed him to succeed on grass and hard courts as well.

Another example is Ratan Tata, the renowned Indian industrialist. Tata was known for his ability to reflect on business strategies and adapt to new market demands. When Tata Motors faced challenges in the global automobile market, instead of sticking to the old ways, Ratan Tata adapted the company's approach, venturing into innovative projects like the Tata Nano and the acquisition of Jaguar Land Rover. His ability to learn, reflect, and pivot in response to industry shifts ensured the continued growth and success of Tata Group.

By reflecting, you become more aware of your strengths and weaknesses, enabling you to set better learning goals and take actions that move you closer to your objectives. Adapting means being flexible, willing to change your methods and approaches based on new information, shifting circumstances, or even changes in your interests and career. The world is evolving, and so should you.

Apply What You Learn

Learning is only half the battle—applying what you learn is where the real magic happens. When you take your newfound knowledge and put it into practice, you're no longer just absorbing information; you're living it. This step transforms theory into experience, and experience is what deepens your understanding and mastery.

Think of it like learning to swim. You can read all the books and watch all the videos about swimming techniques, but it's only when you jump into the water that you truly grasp how to stay afloat, move through the water, and refine your strokes. This is exactly how applying knowledge works. It takes you from a theoretical understanding to a point where the skills become second nature.

For instance, let's say you've just completed a course on digital marketing. The next step is to apply those insights to real-world campaigns—perhaps by running a social media ad for a local business or creating content that's designed to attract more followers. By doing so, you'll not only see what works and what doesn't, but you'll also fine-tune your skills and gain confidence in your ability to execute.

An excellent example is Sundar Pichai, CEO of Google, who often speaks about how hands-on application of technical skills, like programming or design thinking, led to the creation of ground-breaking products like Google Chrome and Android. Instead of just learning concepts, Pichai and his team applied what they knew to real challenges, turning theory into revolutionary tools.

But application doesn't stop at you—it's a two-way street. When you **share your knowledge** with others, not only are you helping them grow, but you're also reinforcing your own understanding. Teaching forces you to explain concepts clearly, which deepens your grasp of the material. Plus, interacting with others can spark new ideas, fresh perspectives, and even a deeper appreciation for the subject.

2.5. Leveraging Feedback for Growth

Leveraging feedback is an essential part of identifying growth opportunities, especially when one is striving to avoid resting on past successes. Feedback, whether from peers, mentors, customers, or stakeholders, provides valuable insights into areas for improvement that may not be immediately apparent. This process involves actively seeking constructive criticism, analyzing patterns in the feedback, and using it to shape personal and professional development.

Let's start by recognizing that feedback highlights blind spots—those areas that may not be visible to you but are clear to others. Whether you're leading a team, running a business, or managing your personal development, feedback reveals patterns and insights you may otherwise miss. For example, customer feedback might point to shifting market demands, urging businesses to innovate before it's too late.

Incorporating feedback into growth strategies helps individuals and organizations stay agile and responsive. For instance, consistent feedback from customers can highlight changing market demands, allowing companies to innovate and adapt their offerings. On a personal level, feedback from colleagues can pinpoint blind spots in leadership or performance, facilitating continuous improvement.

However, for feedback to be effective, one must cultivate a mindset of openness and humility. Rather than perceiving criticism as a threat, it should be viewed as an opportunity to grow and evolve. Regular self-assessments paired with external feedback provide a balanced approach to personal growth, keeping complacency at bay and driving the pursuit of excellence.

The mantra of success is ***learn, earn and learn***. Lifelong learning ensures adaptability in a rapidly evolving world, while setting new goals drives continuous improvement and leverages past achievements for future success. Coupled with a commitment to innovation, this framework enables individuals and organizations to remain competitive, relevant, and forward-thinking. By integrating these strategies, one can effectively navigate challenges, seize new opportunities, and foster enduring growth and achievement. Adopting this holistic approach facilitates not only overcoming current limitations but also shaping a dynamic and prosperous future.

2.6. TOCA: The Cycle of Talent, Opportunity, Continuity, and Attitude

Success is often seen as a combination of talent and opportunity, but there's much more to the equation. **TOCA**—Talent, Opportunity, Continuity, and Attitude—highlights how these elements interact and why neglecting any one of them can lead to failure. Let's dive deeper into this concept and explore how each stage plays a vital role in achieving sustained success.

Talent Without Opportunity

Talent is the raw potential that each person possesses. However, talent alone is not enough. Without the right opportunity to showcase or utilize that talent, it remains dormant, a spark waiting to ignite. Imagine a brilliant musician who has perfected their craft but never gets the chance to perform for an audience. Over time, frustration and self-doubt can set in, leading to disillusionment and a sense of failure. Talent needs a platform—a stage, a project, or even a conversation—to come alive and create impact.

Opportunity Without Continuity

Opportunities are fleeting and require action to make the most of them. If someone seizes an opportunity but fails to maintain momentum, the initial spark fizzles out. Continuity is what transforms an opportunity into lasting success. Picture a budding entrepreneur who lands an investor but doesn't follow through with consistent efforts to build their business. The opportunity slips away, and the dream collapses. Sustained effort—through learning, hard work, and adaptation—is the bridge between opportunity and lasting achievement.

Continuity Without the Right Attitude

Even with talent and continuity, success can crumble if the right attitude isn't maintained. When individuals grow complacent, egotistic, or resistant to change, they sabotage their own progress. Attitude shapes how we perceive challenges, interact with others, and grow from experiences. For instance, a high-performing professional may achieve great milestones but let arrogance creep in, damaging relationships and losing the trust of colleagues. Without humility, adaptability, and gratitude, continuity loses its power, and failure becomes inevitable.

The TOCA framework emphasizes that **true and lasting success is a balance of talent, opportunity, continuity, and attitude**. These elements are interconnected, and neglecting one can disrupt the entire cycle. Talent must meet opportunity, opportunity must be sustained with continuity, and continuity must be driven by the right attitude.

EXERCISES

1. Reflective Journaling

Take 15 minutes to write a reflective journal entry focused on your recent successes and challenges. Answer the following questions:

- What did I learn from my most recent success?
- What challenges did I face, and how did I address them?
- In what ways can I build upon my successes for future growth? This exercise fosters self-awareness and helps identify growth opportunities.

2. Growth Mindset Affirmations

Create a list of affirmations that support a growth mindset. Write at least five statements that challenge limiting beliefs and encourage a focus on learning. For example:

- "I embrace challenges as opportunities to grow."
- "Mistakes are a part of my learning journey." Place these affirmations somewhere visible to remind yourself to maintain a growth-focused perspective.

3. New Goal Brainstorming Session

Set aside time to brainstorm new goals that stretch your capabilities. Use the SMART (Specific, Measurable, Attainable, Relevant and Time Bound) criteria as a guide, and aim to identify at least three new goals.

Discuss these goals with a trusted friend or mentor to gain their insights and refine them further.

4. Feedback Request Challenge

Identify a project or task you've recently completed and request constructive feedback from at least two people (e.g., colleagues, supervisors, or mentors). Prepare specific questions to guide the feedback process, such as:

- What did you think worked well?
- What areas do you believe I could improve upon? Reflect on the feedback received and develop an action plan for addressing any identified areas for improvement.

5. Innovation Scavenger Hunt

Engage in an innovation scavenger hunt by exploring your surroundings—whether at work, home, or in the community. Look for existing products, processes, or services that could be improved or innovated. Document your findings and brainstorm potential improvements or new ideas based on your observations.

6. Set Up a Learning Challenge

Challenge yourself to learn something new within a specific timeframe (e.g., one month). This could involve:

- Enrolling in an online course.
- Attending a workshop or seminar.

- Reading a specific number of books or articles related to your field. Keep track of your progress and reflect on how this new knowledge can be applied to your goals.

Chapter 3: The Power of Perpetual Progress: Embracing Continuous Improvement

3.1. Success Breeds Fear

Success is often seen as the ultimate goal, but for many successful people, it can also be a double-edged sword. With success comes the pressure to maintain it, and ironically, this can lead to a deep-seated fear of failure. This fear can be more intense for those who have achieved significant success because the stakes are higher. Understanding why success can breed fear involves exploring the psychological and social dynamics that make failure feel even more daunting when one is already at the top.

The Pressure to Maintain Success

Once a person has achieved success, there's often an immense pressure to sustain it. This is where the fear of losing status comes into play. According to this sentiment, individuals who have reached a high level of success fear the loss of their status, reputation, and achievements. The higher the success, the greater the fall, and this fear can be paralyzing.

Consider a world-renowned athlete who has won multiple championships. The fear of not living up to past victories can cause anxiety and stress, leading to a performance drop. For instance, many top athletes have expressed fear of not performing well in subsequent games after a major win because the expectation from fans and themselves is so high. *The higher you climb, the harder you fall.* This saying encapsulates the fear of losing everything one has worked hard to achieve, which can be a significant source of anxiety for successful individuals.

A classic example of a sportsperson performing under intense pressure is **MS Dhoni** during the final of the 2011 ICC Cricket World Cup. As the captain of the Indian cricket team, Dhoni was under immense scrutiny and expectations, especially with the tournament being held in India. The nation looked to him to lead the team to victory after 28 long years.

In the final against Sri Lanka, India faced a challenging situation when they lost early wickets during the chase of 275 runs. Dhoni took on the pressure head-on, a decision that surprised many but reflected his belief in taking responsibility during a critical moment. His calm and composed innings of 91 not out, including the iconic match-winning six, not only guided India to a historic win but also showcased his remarkable ability to thrive under extreme pressure.

This example highlights Dhoni's mental toughness, strategic thinking, and exceptional leadership skills, cementing his reputation as one of cricket's greatest finishers and captains. His performance in that final is still celebrated as a defining moment in Indian cricket history.

Success is not final, failure is not fatal: It is the courage to continue that counts.

— Winston Churchill, British Statesman

Churchill's words highlight the importance of resilience and courage in the face of fear, reminding us that both success and failure are parts of a continuous journey.

The Imposter Syndrome

The fear of failure among highly successful individuals often roots itself in a deep psychological experience known as **Imposter Syndrome**. Coined by psychologists Pauline Clance and Suzanne Imes in 1978, this term describes the feeling that you're not as capable as others believe and that you've somehow fooled them into recognizing your success. For those with Imposter Syndrome, accomplishments feel like flukes, and a constant, nagging fear remains: that they will soon be exposed as a fraud. Despite clear success, the person attributes it to luck, timing, or external factors instead of genuine ability.

Consider Sheryl Sandberg, Facebook's former COO and one of the most influential women in tech. Sandberg has revealed how Imposter Syndrome sometimes makes her question her own achievements, despite her groundbreaking impact on the tech industry. She fears that one day people will see through her facade, a fear rooted not in reality but in her internal narrative. Her candid admission brings to light how persistent these doubts can be—even among high achievers with decades of accolades to back up their competence.

Even **Albert Einstein** grappled with these feelings, once confessing, *"The exaggerated esteem in which my lifework is held makes me very ill at ease. I feel compelled to think of myself as an involuntary swindler."*

These examples show that the paradox of success is real: the higher one climbs, the greater the internal pressure to maintain that level of excellence. Instead of bringing relief, each new achievement can amplify the fear of being "found out." Sandberg and Einstein's experiences highlight the idea that Imposter Syndrome doesn't target the untalented; it strikes precisely those who are highly competent but feel the weight of their own expectations, as well as the expectations of others.

In the end, perhaps the takeaway isn't to eliminate these self-doubts but to learn from those who have faced them. When we embrace the vulnerability and discomfort of feeling like an imposter, we give ourselves the freedom to grow. After all, if even a genius like Einstein could embrace his own doubts, surely there's room for all of us to do the same.

The Paradox of Fear of Failure and Success

The Yerkes-Dodson Law is a psychological principle that suggests there is an optimal level of stress or arousal for peak performance. However, too much stress can lead to a decrease in performance. For successful individuals, the fear of failure can push them past this optimal point, leading to a paradox where the fear of failure actually increases the likelihood of failure.

One renowned example of the **Paradox of Fear of Failure and Success** is Michael Jordan, one of the greatest basketball players of all time. Despite his extraordinary success, Jordan often spoke about his intense fear of failure, which drove him to train relentlessly and push himself beyond his limits. However, there were moments when this fear became overwhelming, leading to increased pressure and stress that affected his performance. Although he eventually overcame this, the experience illustrates how even someone as successful as Jordan could be vulnerable to the paradox where fear of failure can lead to performance issues.

Fear is not real. The only place fear can exist is in our thoughts of the future. It is the product of our imagination. Causing us to fear things that do not at present and may not ever exist.

-Michael Jordan

In the business world, successful entrepreneurs often find themselves in a unique psychological dilemma where the very traits that fueled their initial achievements—boldness, innovation, and a willingness to take risks—become tempered by the desire to protect their existing success. This "fear of losing success" can lead to what's often referred to as "status quo bias," where an entrepreneur's mindset shifts from expansion to preservation.

This shift is especially common among business leaders who feel that any misstep could jeopardize the reputation and financial stability they've worked so hard to build. As a result, they become more risk-averse, often avoiding bold, innovative strategies that could expose them to significant loss. While this cautious approach may protect their assets in the short term, it can hinder long-term growth. In rapidly evolving sectors like tech and finance, risk aversion is particularly dangerous, as companies must innovate continuously to remain competitive. A once dynamic business can become sluggish, missing out on emerging opportunities that competitors are quick to seize.

Consider, for instance, a successful tech company that, after its initial growth phase, shifts from pushing technological boundaries to simply iterating on existing products to avoid jeopardizing its core brand. This approach might seem logical to protect its market share, but in an industry that rewards rapid change and innovation, this strategy can backfire. The focus on maintaining current gains over developing new products eventually makes the company vulnerable to more agile startups that embrace risk and meet new market demands.

The irony here is that the very fear of failure—the hesitation to lose what has been built—can pave the way for actual failure in the form of stagnation, loss of market relevance, and eventual decline. In contrast, companies that continue to encourage an entrepreneurial mindset, even at the height of success, often remain resilient. They foster an environment where calculated risks are taken, and innovation is encouraged as a core value, thus keeping the company aligned with emerging trends and consumer needs.

The Cost of Perfectionism

Perfectionism is another psychological factor that can make successful people more afraid of failure. When individuals set unrealistically high standards for themselves, they may fear that any mistake or failure will tarnish their image. This Perfectionism Trap can lead to excessive stress and anxiety, making them less likely to take on new challenges or innovate. The constant pressure to achieve perfection can lead to chronic stress and anxiety. Perfectionists may experience heightened levels of worry about making mistakes or not meeting expectations, which can negatively affect their mental health and overall quality of life. Perfectionism can sometimes lead to decreased performance. The overwhelming pressure to be perfect can result in burnout, decreased motivation, and reduced productivity. The constant self-criticism and fear of failure can undermine confidence and lead to procrastination. Perfectionism can strain relationships with others. Those who impose high standards on themselves may also expect the same from those around them. This can create tension and conflict, as others may feel pressured to meet these unrealistic expectations or feel judged for their own imperfections.

Charlie Chaplin, the iconic comedian, filmmaker, and composer, is a prominent example of someone whose career was deeply influenced by perfectionism. His relentless pursuit of excellence is reflected in his work and his approach to filmmaking. Chaplin was known for his meticulous attention to detail. His films, such as "City Lights," "Modern Times," and "The Great Dictator," are celebrated for their precision in timing, visual composition, and performance. Chaplin's perfectionism drove him to painstakingly refine his work, often spending long hours on every aspect of production to ensure that each element met his high standards. Chaplin's perfectionism led him to innovate and push the boundaries of filmmaking. He often experimented with new techniques and methods to achieve his vision. For example, in "The Gold Rush," he famously performed the "dancing rolls" scene with meticulous choreography, demonstrating his commitment to perfecting even the smallest details of his performances.

Perfection is not attainable, but if we chase perfection, we can catch excellence.

— Vince Lombardi, American Football Coach
Lombardi's quote encourages the pursuit of excellence rather than perfection, reminding us that the fear of not being perfect should not prevent us from striving for success.

Success can paradoxically breed fear, especially the fear of failure. The pressure to maintain success, the imposter syndrome, the paradox of the Yerkes-Dodson Law, and the perfectionism trap all contribute to why successful individuals might fear failure more than others. Understanding these psychological dynamics can help individuals navigate the complex emotions that come with success, allowing them to continue growing and achieving without being paralyzed by fear.

3.2. Embracing Failure as Stepping Stones to Greater Success

Failure is often perceived as the end of the road, a sign of inadequacy or defeat. However, when viewed through the right lens, failure can be one of the most powerful learning tools available. Many successful individuals attribute their achievements not to an absence of failure, but to their ability to learn from it. Embracing failure as a stepping stone to success requires a shift in mindset, supported by psychological theories and real-world examples that demonstrate the transformative power of setbacks.

The Antifragility Theory

Nassim Nicholas Taleb's Antifragility Theory in his book *"Antifragile: Things that can gain from disorder"* offers an intriguing perspective on how we respond to challenges and failures. Unlike resilience, which suggests bouncing back from adversity, antifragility posits that some individuals and systems grow stronger when exposed to stress and challenges.

Let's take an example from animal kingdom that illustrates the concept of adversity leading to growth and resilience. When a baby chick is ready to hatch, it must break through its egg. The process of pecking and pushing through the tough shell is not easy, and it often looks like a struggle. Many people might want to help by cracking the egg open, but doing so would deprive the chick of an essential experience. The effort required to break free strengthens the chick's muscles and prepares it for survival in the outside world. If the chick doesn't go through this struggle, it may not develop the strength it needs to live and grow.

Much like the chick, we face challenges in life that seem overwhelming at first. However, these difficulties build our mental, emotional, and physical resilience. In the same way that the chick's struggle is necessary for its survival, the obstacles we face shape us, teaching us important lessons and giving us the strength to thrive. Through adversity, we don't just survive; we develop the resilience to succeed in the long run.

This example mirrors the idea of **antifragility**, where facing challenges head-on leads to growth, strength, and resilience in the face of future difficulties.

Another example of persistence is Thomas Hunt Morgan, an American scientist who is considered the father of modern genetics. Morgan spent years studying fruit flies (Drosophila melanogaster) in his lab, attempting to uncover the mechanisms of heredity. Early in his research, many of his ideas were met with skepticism, and he faced numerous failures while trying to confirm the hypothesis that genes are located on chromosomes.

Morgan's breakthrough came when he discovered that specific traits were linked to certain chromosomes, proving that genes are carried on chromosomes and laying the foundation for modern genetics. Despite initial setbacks and challenges, Morgan's work eventually earned him the Nobel Prize in Physiology or Medicine in 1933.

Success is not built on success. It's built on failure. It's built on frustration. Sometimes it's built on catastrophe

- Sumner Redstone, Chairman of Paramount Global

This powerful statement challenges the conventional view that success is a linear path, achieved simply by following a smooth, flawless course. Instead, Redstone highlights that real success is often forged through setbacks, struggles, and even total failures.

Rejection as Motivation: The Adversity Quotient

Adversity Quotient (AQ) is a concept developed by Paul Stoltz, which measures a person's ability to deal with adversities in their life. High AQ individuals see rejection and failure as challenges to overcome, rather than reasons to give up. They use setbacks as motivation to push harder and innovate further. Rejection, though often perceived as a setback, can serve as a powerful motivator for personal and professional growth. When individuals encounter rejection, it forces them to confront their shortcomings and re-evaluate their strategies. This process of self-assessment and adjustment is crucial for improvement. Rather than viewing rejection as a failure, it can be seen as an opportunity to refine skills, enhance approaches, and build resilience. The discomfort and frustration of rejection push people out of their comfort zones, encouraging them to innovate and strive for excellence. By learning from the feedback that often accompanies rejection, individuals can make informed changes and strengthen their efforts. Additionally, rejection can ignite a renewed sense of purpose, driving individuals to overcome challenges and prove their critics wrong. Embracing rejection as a catalyst for growth fosters a mindset that values persistence and adaptability, ultimately leading to greater success and fulfilment.

J.K. Rowling, the author of the Harry Potter series, faced numerous rejections from publishers before finally being accepted. Instead of being discouraged, Rowling used the rejections as motivation to improve her manuscript and continue her pursuit of publication. Today, she is one of the most successful authors in the world, illustrating how rejection can fuel determination and lead to greater success.

In this quote Rowling explains, how reaching a low point can serve as a transformative catalyst for positive change and growth.

The Iterative Learning Process

The Iterative Learning Process is a concept from educational psychology that emphasizes learning through repetition and refinement. Each failure or mistake provides valuable feedback that can be used to improve future attempts. This process is particularly relevant in fields like entrepreneurship, where trial and error are often necessary components of innovation. In entrepreneurship, for example, a startup may test different business models or marketing strategies multiple times. Each iteration helps to identify what works and what doesn't, gradually honing the approach to better meet market needs.

Dyson's founder, Sir James Dyson, went through 5,126 failed prototypes before successfully creating the first bagless vacuum cleaner. Each failure provided critical insights that ultimately led to the final product. Dyson's perseverance and willingness to embrace failure as a learning tool resulted in a product that revolutionized the vacuum cleaner industry.

Embracing failure as a learning tool is crucial for personal and professional growth. The growth mindset, adversity quotient, resilience, and iterative learning process all illustrate how failure can be transformed into a stepping stone toward greater success. By viewing failures not as endpoints but as opportunities for improvement, individuals can unlock their full potential and achieve their goals.

3.3. Techniques to Stay Resilient in the Face of Setbacks

Resilience is the ability to bounce back from adversity, maintain focus, and continue pursuing goals despite setbacks. It's not about avoiding challenges but rather about developing the strength to overcome them. Building resilience is crucial for anyone striving for long-term success, as life inevitably presents obstacles that can test our resolve. There are several techniques, supported by psychological theories and real-life examples, that can help individuals cultivate resilience.

The Resilience Theory

Resilience theory, a concept rooted in psychological and developmental research, highlights the ability of individuals to recover from setbacks, adapt to change, and persevere in the face of adversity. According to the **Transactional Model of Stress and Coping by Lazarus and Folkman,** resilience is not a static trait but a dynamic process that involves how individuals perceive and respond to stressors. This theory suggests that resilient people are those who manage stress effectively by using adaptive coping strategies and viewing challenges as opportunities for growth rather than threats. They understand that failure is a natural and inevitable part of life's journey, and they leverage these experiences as valuable learning tools.

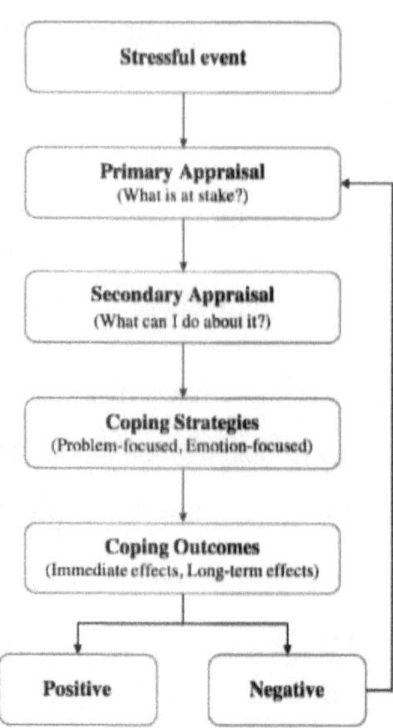

Transactional Model of Stress and Coping

By reframing setbacks as opportunities for personal development, individuals can maintain motivation and adapt their strategies to overcome obstacles. The concept of resilience thus emphasizes the importance of a growth mindset, where failure is seen not as a reflection of one's abilities but as a stepping stone towards greater success and personal evolution. This perspective is supported by research in positive psychology, which underscores that resilience fosters not only survival but also thriving and success in the face of adversity.

Let's take the example of Indian Actor Amitabh Bachchan. His journey through adversity exemplifies remarkable resilience and the ability to bounce back from significant setbacks. Despite initial struggles and rejection in the early years of his career—where he was criticized for his height and voice and faced numerous auditions without success—Bachchan's perseverance eventually led to his breakthrough with the film

Zanjeer in 1973. However, his career faced another major challenge in the 1980s when he experienced a period of decline due to a series of box office failures and a near-fatal accident on the set of *Coolie*. Rather than succumbing to these difficulties, Bachchan demonstrated exceptional resilience by reinventing himself, embracing new roles, and even entering the world of television with the successful quiz show *Kaun Banega Crorepati (Who wants to be billionaire)*. His ability to adapt, persevere, and thrive despite these adversities underscores his profound resilience and dedication to his craft, solidifying his status as a legendary figure in Indian cinema.

Nelson Mandela's resilience during his 27 years of imprisonment is a powerful example of how support systems can help build resilience. Mandela remained connected to his supporters and the global community, which provided him with the strength to endure his hardships and continue his fight against apartheid.

The greatest glory in living lies not in never falling, but in rising every time we fall.

- Nelson Mandela,

President of South Africa [1994 A.D. to 1999 A.D.]

This quote reflects a deep understanding of the human experience, resilience, and the transformative power of perseverance. This powerful statement speaks to the essential nature of overcoming challenges and the importance of tenacity in the face of adversity.

Resilience Theory highlights the role of social support systems in helping individuals navigate adversity. According to this theory, people who have strong relationships with family, friends, and mentors are more likely to be resilient because they can draw on these connections for emotional support, guidance, and encouragement.

The Power of Positive Thinking: Cognitive Behavioral Theory

Cognitive Behavioral Theory (CBT), developed by Aaron Beck in the 1960s, emphasizes the role of positive thinking in managing stress and overcoming challenges. CBT suggests that our thoughts influence our emotions and behaviors. By reframing negative thoughts into positive ones, individuals can change their emotional responses to setbacks and build resilience.

Ashleigh Barty, the Australian tennis player. Barty faced numerous challenges throughout her career, including the pressures of professional tennis, injuries, and periods of self-doubt. However, instead of succumbing to these challenges, she used positive thinking and mental strategies to overcome them. In particular, Barty has spoken about how she learned to reframe negative thoughts and maintain a resilient mindset, focusing on what she could control — her attitude and effort — rather than worrying about outcomes.

Her ability to stay calm and positive, even during setbacks, played a key role in her eventual rise to world No. 1 and winning prestigious titles like Wimbledon. Barty's journey exemplifies how Cognitive Behavioral Theory can help athletes overcome mental barriers, by changing negative thought patterns and building resilience in the face of challenges.

Yesterday I was clever, so I wanted to change the world. Today I am wise, so I am changing myself.

> *- Jalal ad-Din Muhammad Rumi[13th century, Persian Poet]*

The above quote reflects a profound shift in perspective from external ambition to internal growth. It speaks to the idea that wisdom is not about seeking to control or change the world around us but about understanding and transforming ourselves first.

The 3 Cs of Hardiness: Commitment, Control, and Challenge

Psychologists Suzanne Kobasa and Salvatore Maddi introduced the concept of Hardiness, which consists of three key components: ***Commitment, Control, and Challenge.*** Hardy individuals are committed to their goals, believe they have control over their circumstances, and view challenges as opportunities for growth rather than threats.

Commitment: Staying dedicated to your goals, even when faced with difficulties.

Control: Believing in your ability to influence outcomes through your actions.

Challenge: Viewing setbacks as opportunities to learn and grow.

Richard Branson, the founder of the Virgin Group, exemplifies the three Cs of hardiness. His commitment to his vision, belief in his ability to control his destiny, and willingness to embrace challenges have led him to create a global business empire. Branson has faced numerous setbacks, including failed ventures, but his hardy attitude has enabled him to bounce back stronger each time.

Do not be embarrassed by your failures, learn from them and start again

- Richard Branson, Founder of Virgin Group

Michael Jordan's journey to becoming a basketball legend is a powerful testament to the importance of a growth mindset—a concept popularized by psychologist Carol Dweck. Despite facing significant setbacks, including being cut from his high school basketball team, Jordan transformed his initial disappointment into a driving force for improvement.

In 1978, Jordan was not selected for the varsity basketball team. Instead of succumbing to despair, he used this rejection as fuel to hone his skills. He practiced tirelessly, often playing in the backyard until late at night, determined to become a better player. This dedication paid off when he made the team the following year and quickly established himself as a standout player.

Jordan's growth mindset was evident throughout his career. He embraced challenges, sought feedback, and viewed failures as opportunities for learning. His relentless work ethic and discipline helped him improve his game continuously, both in practice and during games.

I've missed more than 9,000 shots in my career. I've lost almost 300 games. 26 times, I've been trusted to take the game-winning shot and missed. I've failed over and over and over again in my life. And that is why I succeed

— Michael Jordan, Former Professional Basketball Player

Jordan's impact extends beyond basketball. He revolutionized the game and the business of sports through his competitive spirit and innovative marketing strategies, including the iconic Air Jordan brand. His success is often attributed to his ability to adapt and grow, both as an athlete and as a person. The lessons he learned about perseverance and resilience resonate with individuals in various fields, illustrating that setbacks can be stepping stones to greatness.

Jordan's story is a reminder that a growth mindset can lead to extraordinary achievements, reinforcing the idea that with hard work, determination, and the willingness to learn from failure, one can overcome obstacles and reach new heights.

3.4. The Importance of Self-Compassion

Self-Compassion Theory, developed by Kristin Neff, suggests that treating oneself with kindness and understanding during times of failure or hardship can build resilience. Instead of being overly critical or harsh, self-compassion allows individuals to acknowledge their struggles without judgment, leading to greater emotional strength and recovery from setbacks. Self-compassion has practical benefits in everyday life. For example, athletes can use self-compassion to recover from losses and injuries, which helps them refocus on training rather than dwelling on failures. In the workplace, professionals who practice self-compassion can navigate challenges more easily, leading to a healthier work environment.

It always seems impossible until it's done.

- Nelson Mandela,

President of South Africa [1994 A.D. to 1999 A.D.]

Arianna Huffington, the founder of The Huffington Post, experienced a public and personal collapse due to exhaustion. Instead of pushing herself harder, she embraced self-compassion, allowing herself to recover and eventually become an advocate for well-being and resilience in the workplace.

Failure is not the opposite of success; it's part of success

— Arianna Huffington, American Author

Building resilience is essential for navigating life's inevitable challenges. Whether through positive thinking, embracing a hardy attitude, relying on support systems, fostering a growth mindset, or practicing self-compassion, individuals can develop the resilience needed to overcome setbacks and continue pursuing their goals. By adopting these techniques, you can turn adversity into an opportunity for growth and, ultimately, success.

In conclusion, the fear of failure often intensifies with success due to the pressure to maintain achievements, the prevalence of imposter syndrome, and the paradoxical effects of stress on performance. Successful individuals may face a unique set of challenges, where the stakes are higher and the fear of losing status or reputation becomes more pronounced. However, understanding these psychological dynamics is crucial for managing and overcoming this fear. Embracing failure as a learning tool, as advocated by the growth mindset and iterative learning process, can transform setbacks into opportunities for growth. By viewing failures not as the end but as stepping stones to success, individuals can cultivate resilience and continue to thrive. Moreover, the pursuit of excellence rather than perfection, coupled with a high adversity quotient, can help navigate the complex emotions tied to success. Ultimately, success and failure are intertwined, and those who master the art of learning from failures are better equipped to sustain long-term success and personal growth.

EXERCISES

1. Fear-Setting Exercise: Address the fear that comes with success and examine its roots.

Activity - Write down your biggest fear related to your current success. Break it down into three columns:

- What's the worst that could happen?
- What steps can you take to prevent this from happening?
- If the worst happens, how can you recover?

Reflect on how this exercise changes your perspective on your fear.

2. Failure Reflection Journal: Embrace failure as a stepping stone.

Activity - Keep a journal where you document recent setbacks or failures. For each entry, write down:

- What happened?
- What did you learn from it?
- How can you apply this lesson in the future?

Review your entries monthly to track your growth and resilience.

3. Resilience Challenge - Develop techniques to stay resilient.

Activity: Choose a recent setback you faced

- Identify three coping strategies you used to navigate it.
- Reflect on how effective these strategies were.
- Write a plan to incorporate at least one new resilience technique (like mindfulness or positive affirmations) into your routine for the next month.

4. Self-Compassion Letter: Foster self-compassion.

Activity: Write a letter to yourself addressing a recent struggle or failure. In this letter, include:

- Acknowledgment of your feelings.
- Kind words of encouragement, as if you were writing to a friend.
- Specific actions you will take to move forward with compassion.
- Keep this letter somewhere you can revisit it whenever you need a reminder to practice self-compassion.

5. Group Sharing Session: Share experiences and learn from others.

Activity: Organize a small group discussion or support circle with peers or colleagues.

- Each person shares a failure they have experienced and how they learned from it.
- Discuss how embracing failure has led to growth and share strategies for resilience.
- Record key insights and action steps to implement in your lives.

Chapter 4: Shifting Gears: Mastering Adaptability in a Fast-Paced World

4.1. The Inescapable Nature of Change

In a world characterized by rapid technological advancements and shifting societal norms, adaptability has become a critical trait for success. The ability to adjust to new circumstances and embrace change is essential for both personal and professional growth. Theories from psychology and business, alongside real-life examples from Japan, illustrate why adaptability is crucial in navigating a constantly evolving landscape.

Heraclitus, the ancient Greek philosopher, famously declared, *"The only constant in life is change"*. This observation remains profoundly relevant in our modern era, where change is an integral part of everyday life. In Japan, this concept is embodied in the principle of kaizen, which means "continuous improvement." This philosophy underpins Japan's approach to personal and organizational development, emphasizing that incremental improvements and adaptability can lead to substantial long-term success.

Toyota's implementation of the Kaizen philosophy in its production processes revolutionized the automotive industry. By encouraging small, continuous improvements and empowering employees to suggest changes, Toyota increased efficiency and quality, setting a benchmark for global manufacturing standards. This adaptability and commitment to incremental progress have been key to Toyota's long-term success.

Improvement is the essence of change.

- Akio Toyoda, President of Toyota Motor Corporation

This quote captures a core principle that has driven Toyota's success: the continuous pursuit of improvement as the foundation for meaningful change. This mindset is closely aligned with Toyota's famous Kaizen philosophy, which focuses on continuous, incremental improvements across all levels of the organization, from manufacturing processes to management practices.

4.2. The Theory of Evolution: Survival of the Fittest

Charles Darwin's theory of evolution, which posits that survival depends on an organism's ability to adapt to its environment, can be applied to businesses and individuals. In the context of modern Japan, companies that have successfully adapted to technological and market changes exemplify this principle.

A great example of personal adaptability from the world of West Indian sports is the legendary cricketer Sir Garfield Sobers. Sobers, hailing from Barbados, started his cricketing career as a bowler but soon developed into one of the greatest all-rounders the game has ever seen. His ability to excel in multiple roles within cricket, from fast bowler to spin bowler to one of the most dominant batsmen, exemplifies his adaptability—a trait crucial for survival and success in the ever-evolving landscape of sports.

Sobers' evolution throughout his career mirrors Darwin's theory, as he continuously adapted his game to stay at the top. Initially known for his bowling prowess, he worked hard to improve his batting, culminating in his record-breaking score of 365 in a Test match in 1958, which remained the highest individual score for several years. His versatility in changing roles within the game, combined with his leadership qualities as the West Indies captain, ensured his long-standing relevance and success in cricket. His adaptability across different facets of the game showcases how an individual, like any organism in Darwin's theory, must evolve to maintain success in changing environments. Sobers remains a symbol of growth, innovation, and survival through versatility.

Innovation is the ability to see change as an opportunity, not a threat.

- Steve Jobs, American Businessman

A well-known Japanese example of adaptability is Tadashi Yanai, the founder and CEO of Fast Retailing, the parent company of UNIQLO. Yanai's ability to adapt and evolve his business strategy has made UNIQLO one of the largest clothing retailers in the world.

Initially, Yanai started with a chain of men's tailoring shops inherited from his father, but he soon realized that the company needed to adapt to changing consumer preferences. Yanai transformed the business model, shifting focus from tailoring to casual wear, and rebranded it as UNIQLO (Unique Clothing Warehouse). He adopted a global mindset, investing heavily in technology and streamlining the supply chain to keep costs low while maintaining high-quality products.

UNIQLO also demonstrated adaptability in its approach to international markets. Unlike many Japanese companies that struggled overseas, Yanai made strategic partnerships and localized his approach to suit various regions while maintaining the brand's core identity. For example, in China and the U.S., he tailored store designs and product offerings to fit the specific tastes and cultural needs of each market.

Tadashi Yanai's success with UNIQLO reflects how adaptability, openness to innovation, and a growth-oriented mindset can drive long-term success in a competitive global market.

4.3. The Growth Mindset: Embracing Change for Continuous Learning

Carol Dweck's Growth Mindset theory, which emphasizes that abilities can be developed through effort and learning, is integral to adaptability. In Japan, this mindset is reflected in the educational and corporate cultures, where continuous learning and adaptability are highly valued.

Fuji Kindergarten is a groundbreaking school located in Tokyo, Japan, renowned for its innovative architectural design and educational philosophy aimed at nurturing adaptability, creativity, and independence in young children. The kindergarten was designed by the architecture firm Tezuka Architects, led by Takaharu Tezuka and Yui Tezuka, and it opened in 2007. The school is unique in its design—built as a large, oval-shaped building with an open rooftop that acts as a continuous play area for the children. The architecture was specifically created to encourage freedom of movement and interaction with nature, allowing the children to develop adaptability through exploration.

One of the core philosophies behind Fuji Kindergarten is that children should be given the freedom to make their own decisions, explore their surroundings, and solve problems without too much adult intervention. This approach is designed to build resilience and adaptability in students by giving them control over their learning environment. The open design of the building, where children can run across the rooftop or slide down to the ground level, fosters a sense of independence and flexibility.

Additionally, Fuji Kindergarten incorporates the idea of "learning by doing," where children are constantly interacting with their environment, whether it be through physical activities, social interactions, or spontaneous play. The absence of walls and barriers within the school allows children to experience freedom and encourages them to adapt to varying scenarios as they navigate different parts of the school. This method of education is aimed at making children more adaptable to change, an essential skill in today's ever-evolving world.

The greatest enemy of progress is not stagnation, but false progress

-Sydney J. Harris, American Journalist

Harris's quote very well with Fuji Kindergarten's teaching model. Fuji Kindergarten ensures that the learning is real and adaptive, not just a superficial achievement of milestones. False progress, in this context, could be represented by standardized, rote learning that doesn't prepare children for future challenges. The school's approach avoids this pitfall by developing skills like problem-solving, resilience, and adaptability—elements crucial for genuine progress in a constantly evolving world. Just like true progress demands constant learning and adaptation, Fuji Kindergarten instills these values in its young students, ensuring their development is both authentic and future-oriented.

4.4. The Psychological Flexibility Model: Adapting to Emotional and Situational Changes

Psychological flexibility, a key principle from Acceptance and Commitment Therapy (ACT), emphasizes the ability to remain present and adjust behaviors in line with one's core values. This concept plays a vital role in managing stress and effectively navigating life's challenges. In Japan, the cultural emphasis on emotional resilience and adaptability offers a profound illustration of psychological flexibility in action.

Central to this concept is **IKIGAI**, the Japanese notion of finding purpose and meaning in life. As Hector Garcia and Francesc Miralles succinctly put it, *"Your IKIGAI is the reason you wake up in the morning."* When individuals identify and embrace their IKIGAI, they develop a powerful sense of purpose that guides their actions and decisions. This sense of direction equips them to adapt to life's inevitable changes with grace and resilience.

For example, consider a Japanese artisan, such as a master potter who loses his studio in a natural disaster. Instead of succumbing to despair, he reflects on his IKIGAI—the joy of creating and sharing beautiful pottery. This clarity of purpose enables him to pivot, perhaps by experimenting with new techniques or collaborating with other artisans. His adaptability not only helps him recover but also enriches his craft, illustrating how a strong sense of IKIGAI fosters resilience.

Moreover, studies have shown that individuals who embrace their IKIGAI often experience lower stress levels and greater overall well-being. This aligns with the values deeply ingrained in Japanese culture, where the pursuit of meaning encourages a mindset that welcomes change rather than resists it.

By cultivating psychological flexibility through the lens of IKIGAI, individuals can navigate life's ups and downs with a renewed sense of purpose. Embracing this philosophy not only enhances personal growth but also contributes to a more resilient and fulfilled life—one that is rich with meaning and adaptability.

4.5. The Agile Methodology: Adaptability in Action

The Agile Methodology emphasizes iterative progress, collaboration, and flexibility. While it originated in the software industry, its principles have been adopted by various sectors in Japan to enhance adaptability and responsiveness.

One remarkable example of adaptability in the music industry from India is **A.R. Rahman**. Known as the "Mozart of Madras", Rahman has consistently evolved his music style to remain relevant in a rapidly changing industry.

Starting his career in the early 1990s with soundtracks that blended traditional Indian music with contemporary elements, Rahman has embraced various genres, including pop, classical, and electronic music. His ability to incorporate different musical styles and technologies has kept him at the forefront of the global music scene. For instance, his work on the soundtrack for the film "Slumdog Millionaire" not only won him international acclaim but also introduced Indian music to a global audience, showcasing his adaptability to various cultural contexts.

Rahman's innovative approach extends beyond just music composition. He has collaborated with various artists across genres and borders, which has allowed him to experiment and grow. His willingness to embrace change and push boundaries exemplifies how adaptability can lead to sustained success.

Agile is not a goal, but a way of thinking and working that evolves with the times.

- Jeff Sutherland, Creators of Scrum

Adaptability is a critical skill in navigating today's rapidly changing world. Drawing on theories like Darwin's evolution, Dweck's growth mindset, and psychological flexibility, highlights the importance of being adaptable. Embracing change, continuous learning, and maintaining a flexible approach can transform challenges into opportunities for growth and innovation.

4.6. Strategies for Staying Flexible: Cultivating a Mindset of Adaptability

Flexibility is a cornerstone of adaptability, allowing individuals and organizations to navigate change effectively and seize new opportunities. Cultivating a mindset of adaptability involves more than just reacting to change; it requires proactive strategies to remain agile and resilient. Some of the ways in which you can adapt flexibility are:

Embrace the Concept of Psychological Flexibility

Psychological flexibility is the ability to remain open to new experiences, thoughts, and emotions while staying focused on long-term goals and values. This adaptability is essential for effectively navigating changing circumstances and overcoming challenges. To implement psychological flexibility, begin by practicing mindfulness. This involves engaging in activities that help you stay present and aware of your thoughts and feelings without allowing them to dictate your actions.

A powerful example of psychological flexibility in tennis can be seen in **Novak Djokovic,** one of the sport's all-time greats. Djokovic's journey to the top of the tennis world exemplifies his ability to adapt to challenges while maintaining a focus on his long-term goals and values.

In the early years of his career, Djokovic faced significant pressure and scrutiny, particularly regarding his physical fitness and mental resilience. After struggling with injuries and fluctuating performances, he realized that to achieve sustained success, he needed to fundamentally change his approach. This transformation involved adopting a holistic view of his training, which included physical conditioning, mental coaching, and dietary changes.

One of the most notable aspects of Djokovic's adaptability is his emphasis on mindfulness and meditation. He began practicing mindfulness techniques to enhance his focus and emotional regulation during matches. This mental training allowed him to stay present, manage stress effectively, and bounce back from setbacks, such as his unexpected loss at the 2016 French Open, where he was heavily favored to win.

Djokovic's ability to embrace change and integrate new practices into his training routine demonstrates psychological flexibility. His commitment to continuous learning and improvement has led him to become a multiple Grand Slam champion, and he frequently adapts his game strategies based on his opponents and conditions.

His story is a testament to the idea that psychological flexibility, combined with dedication and hard work, can lead to remarkable achievements in the face of adversity. As Djokovic himself said, "I am not afraid of anything. I just want to play my best tennis," showcasing his focus on long-term goals despite the inevitable challenges that come his way.

Novak Djokovic's journey in the world of tennis perfectly illustrates Charles Darwin's quote: "It is not the strongest of the species that survive, nor the most intelligent, but the one most responsive to change." Djokovic's ability to adapt his training regimen, mindset, and strategies to overcome challenges demonstrates the essence of psychological flexibility.

Foster a Culture of Experimentation

Encouraging experimentation requires fostering an environment where trying new approaches and learning from failures are central to the process. This mindset nurtures innovation and flexibility. Madam Marie Curie is a perfect example of someone who adopted a philosophy of experimentation and achieved remarkable success through her pioneering work in radioactivity. Born in Poland in 1867, Curie faced numerous challenges, including societal barriers to women in science. Nevertheless, she persevered, driven by a deep curiosity and a commitment to understanding the nature of radiation.

Curie's groundbreaking research involved rigorous experimentation. She famously isolated the radioactive elements polonium and radium, despite working in rudimentary laboratory conditions without the safety precautions we have today. Her relentless pursuit of knowledge was exemplified by her quote, "One never notices what has been done; one can only see what remains to be done." This mindset of continuous learning and experimentation allowed her to make significant contributions to science, ultimately earning her two Nobel Prizes in Physics and Chemistry—an unparalleled achievement that still inspires scientists today.

The only real mistake is the one from which we learn nothing

- Henry Ford, American Industrialist

Curie's approach highlights the importance of fostering a culture of experimentation. She viewed challenges not as obstacles but as opportunities to learn and innovate. By embracing risks and learning from failures, Curie's work not only advanced scientific understanding but also paved the way for future generations of scientists, particularly women.

Develop Strategic Agility

Strategic agility entails the capacity to swiftly adjust strategies and actions in response to evolving conditions, combining foresight, flexibility, and rapid decision-making. To implement this, begin by conducting regular environmental scans to continuously monitor and analyze external factors that could affect your business or personal goals. This ongoing assessment helps you stay informed about changes and anticipate potential impacts. Additionally, develop strategic plans with built-in flexibility. These plans should allow for adjustments based on new information or shifting circumstances, enabling you to adapt quickly and effectively as conditions evolve. By integrating these practices, you can enhance your ability to remain agile and responsive in a dynamic environment. Strategic agility emphasizes the importance of being able to pivot and adapt strategies quickly in response to market dynamics.

The famous "boiling frog" story illustrates the danger of failing to adapt to slow, incremental changes. If you place a frog in boiling water, it will jump out immediately. However, if you place it in cold water and slowly raise the temperature, the frog will remain in the water, unaware of the gradual changes, until it's too late. The lesson is clear: to survive and thrive, you must remain vigilant and adaptable to both sudden and gradual changes. By cultivating flexibility and staying alert to your environment, you can avoid complacency and effectively navigate the shifts and challenges that come your way.

This metaphor serves as a reminder that we must continually assess and adjust to both large and small changes, ensuring that we don't fall into a trap of comfort or stagnation. Flexibility, both psychological and strategic, allows us to remain adaptable and avoid being caught unaware by subtle shifts in our circumstances.

Cultivate Emotional Intelligence

Cultivating emotional intelligence (EI) is like equipping yourself with a superpower that helps you navigate the intricate landscape of human interactions and adapt to life's ever-changing circumstances. EI isn't just about understanding your own emotions; it's about harnessing that understanding to improve your relationships and decision-making.

To kickstart your journey toward greater emotional intelligence, begin with self-awareness. Regularly reflect on your emotional responses to various situations—what triggers joy, frustration, or anxiety? This reflective practice allows you to recognize patterns in your feelings, empowering you to make more conscious decisions. Consider journaling about your emotions or practicing mindfulness techniques to enhance this self-awareness. As you become more in tune with your feelings, you'll find it easier to manage them effectively.

Next up, it's time to sharpen your social skills. Effective communication, empathy, and relationship-building are the cornerstones of EI. Engage in active listening—really pay attention to what others are saying and strive to understand their perspectives. This not only fosters deeper connections but also helps you respond thoughtfully rather than react impulsively. Get involved in group activities, join clubs, or volunteer in your community. These experiences expose you to diverse individuals and viewpoints, providing invaluable opportunities to practice and refine your social abilities.

Nelson Mandela is a profound example of emotional intelligence (EI) in action, particularly evident during his leadership as South Africa transitioned from apartheid to democracy. After enduring 27 years of imprisonment, Mandela emerged not embittered by his experiences but rather committed to reconciliation and unity. This remarkable ability to empathize with both his supporters and former oppressors exemplifies a key aspect of EI: the capacity to understand and connect with the emotions of others, even in the face of deep societal divides.

Mandela's emotional resilience played a crucial role in navigating the complex landscape of post-apartheid South Africa. Instead of seeking revenge, he advocated for forgiveness, knowing that true progress could only be achieved through understanding and collaboration. His famous quote, "I never lose. I either win or learn," highlights his belief that setbacks can be transformed into opportunities for growth. This mindset reflects a profound understanding of the importance of adaptability—an essential component of emotional intelligence.

As noted by Daniel Goleman, a leading expert on emotional intelligence, the ability to manage one's emotions and the emotions of others is vital for effective leadership. Goleman emphasizes that emotional intelligence not only helps individuals cope with stress but also enables them to navigate complex social environments with composure and empathy. Mandela's approach to leadership showcased how EI can facilitate dialogue, promote healing, and build bridges in communities marked by conflict.

Build and Leverage Support Networks

Having a robust support network is pivotal for enhancing adaptability and problem-solving skills, as it offers invaluable resources, diverse perspectives, and emotional support during challenging times. To create this network, one should begin by strategically networking with mentors, peers, and industry experts who can provide guidance and support. Engaging in professional associations, attending industry events, and participating in community forums can facilitate these connections. According to social network theory, leveraging social connections allows individuals to access crucial information and resources, which can significantly aid in adaptability.

Additionally, it's essential to actively seek diverse perspectives by interacting with individuals from various backgrounds and fields. This exposure broadens understanding and enhances innovative problem-solving approaches. Engaging in collaborative projects or cross-disciplinary initiatives can enrich one's viewpoint and spark new ideas. Research suggests that diverse teams often outperform homogeneous groups due to the variety of perspectives they bring to the table.

A prime example of leveraging a support network is Richard Branson, the founder of the Virgin Group. Branson emphasizes the importance of his extensive network of advisors and collaborators, stating that it has been instrumental to his success. By surrounding himself with individuals from diverse backgrounds, he has gained unique insights and support, allowing him to navigate challenges more effectively. His ability to embrace different viewpoints has helped him innovate and adapt in the competitive business landscape.

Surround yourself with only people who are going to lift you higher

- Oprah Winfrey, American Host and Television Producer

In essence, cultivating a strong support network, characterized by strategic relationships and diverse perspectives, not only enhances adaptability but also fosters resilience and creativity in problem-solving.

Stay connected to your passion

Staying connected to your passion is vital for sustaining the long-term enthusiasm and drive needed to excel in your work. Staying connected to your passion is the secret sauce that fuels long-term enthusiasm and excellence in your work. When you nurture the motivations that ignited your journey, you keep the flames of commitment alive, propelling you toward ongoing excellence. Passion Theory, articulated by **Vallerand et al. (2003)**, highlights that passion is a significant predictor of engagement and performance. Essentially, when you remain tied to what you love, motivation flows freely, and your drive intensifies. Engaging in activities related to your passion not only keeps the excitement alive but also ensures you remain inspired.

Take Michael Jordan as a quintessential example. Even after establishing himself as one of the greatest basketball players of all time, Jordan didn't ***rest on his laurels***. He pushed himself to improve, famously returning to the NBA after a brief retirement. This bold move was a testament to his growth mindset and relentless pursuit of excellence, as detailed in the book *I Can't Accept Not Trying: Michael Jordan on the Pursuit of Excellence* (Jordan & Kariuki, 1994).

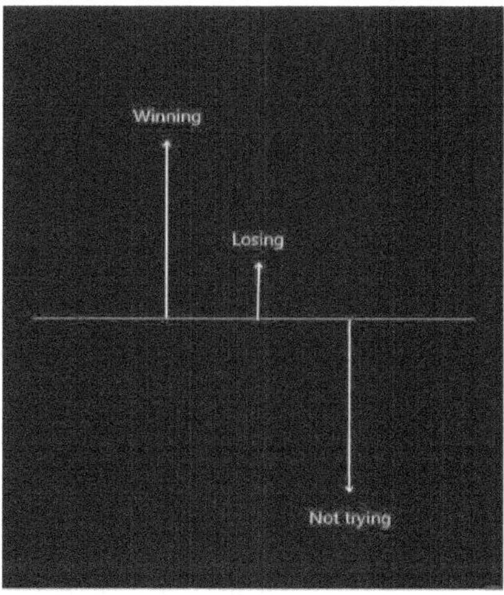

In the above figure, **Winning**, **Losing**, and **Not Trying** are not just outcomes—they're mindsets that define how we approach challenges in life. To win is to persist despite the odds, to rise above comfort, and to push yourself beyond what feels safe or easy. Winning is not just about crossing the finish line first; it's about giving your best effort and proving to yourself that growth is possible. When you win, it's a reflection of your dedication, preparation, and the courage to keep moving forward, no matter how difficult the path may seem.

Losing, on the other hand, is often misunderstood. Losing is not failure in the true sense; it's a stepping stone. Every loss teaches lessons that success cannot. It uncovers weaknesses, builds resilience, and forces you to confront what went wrong so you can improve. Losing is valuable because it means you tried—it means you stepped out of your comfort zone and gave yourself a chance to grow.

But not trying? That's the real failure. Not trying stems from fear—fear of failure, fear of judgment, or fear of stepping outside the safety of what you know. It's resting on your laurels, convincing yourself that staying comfortable is better than risking a loss. However, by not trying, you rob yourself of the opportunity to learn, grow, and achieve something greater.

The essence of *"Don't Rest on Your Laurels"* lies in understanding these differences. Life is not about avoiding losses or staying in the comfort zone; it's about embracing the effort and growth that come with trying. Winning may bring joy, losing may bring wisdom, but not trying leaves you stagnant. Don't let fear hold you back—your best performance is always ahead of you, and the only way to reach it is to step into the arena and give it your all.

Moreover, according to **Self-Determination Theory (Deci & Ryan, 1985),** intrinsic motivation—often driven by personal goals and values—is crucial for maintaining long-term engagement and success. Ambition, a form of intrinsic motivation, fuels your commitment and enthusiasm for your work. In an age where distractions abound, connecting with your passion can be your secret weapon against stagnation. So, embrace your passions, reflect on your purpose, and let the intrinsic drive of ambition lead you to uncharted territories of achievement.

In the end, the journey becomes a celebration of passion and ambition, illustrating that success isn't just about reaching the destination; it's about thriving on the path of continuous growth and fulfillment. After all, the world is waiting for your unique contribution—so stay passionate and let your drive take flight!

The only limit to our realization of tomorrow is our doubts of today

-Franklin D. Roosevelt, US President [1933 AD to 1945 AD]

In conclusion, cultivating adaptability is crucial for thriving in a dynamic world. By embracing psychological flexibility, fostering a culture of experimentation, developing strategic agility, enhancing emotional intelligence, and building a strong support network, individuals and organizations can effectively navigate change and seize opportunities. These strategies enable proactive responses to evolving circumstances, promote innovative thinking, and support resilient problem-solving. As a result, adaptability becomes a powerful tool for achieving long-term success and maintaining a competitive edge in an ever-changing environment.

EXERCISES

1. Change Reflection Journal: This exercise helps you recognize your adaptability and learn from each experience, fostering a growth mindset.

Activity: Keep a weekly journal focused on changes you've experienced, both big and small. Reflect on how you felt about these changes and how you adapted to them.

- What changes did I encounter this week?
- How did I react initially?
- What strategies did I use to adapt?
- What did I learn from this experience?

2. Adaptability Role-Play: This exercise encourages you to think on your feet and develop strategies for managing change effectively.

Activity: Partner with a friend or colleague and engage in role-playing scenarios that require adaptability. Choose scenarios that reflect changes you might encounter in your personal or professional life. Examples:

- Sudden changes in a project deadline.
- Receiving unexpected feedback on a presentation.
- Transitioning to a new team structure.

3. Mindfulness Practice: This practice enhances your emotional regulation, which is essential for adaptability.

Activity: Dedicate 10-15 minutes daily to mindfulness meditation. Focus on observing your thoughts and feelings without judgment, particularly when thinking about change. Use guided meditation apps or videos that focus on building resilience and flexibility in the face of change.

4. Agile Mindset Workshop: This hands-on experience helps you understand and practice adaptability in a structured environment.

Activity: Organize or participate in a workshop that focuses on agile methodologies in your field. Collaborate with peers to simulate an agile project, adapting to changes as they arise. Components:

- Short sprints of project work.

- Regular feedback loops.

- Adaptive planning sessions.

5. Flexibility Challenge: This exercise pushes you out of your comfort zone and builds your adaptability muscle.

Activity: Set a "Flexibility Challenge" for yourself each week. Choose an area in your life where you can be more adaptable. Examples:

- Try a new approach to a routine task.

- Change your usual schedule.

- Engage with people outside your comfort zone.

These exercises aim to enhance your adaptability and resilience in an ever-changing world. Embrace the challenges and insights that come with each activity, and watch how your ability to navigate change flourishes!

Chapter 5: Building a Lasting Legacy: How to Ensure Your Success is Sustained Over Time

5.1. The Power of Mentorship in Personal Growth

Effective leadership extends beyond directing and managing; it involves setting a personal example that inspires and motivates others to continuously strive for excellence. Leaders who embody a commitment to growth and resilience encourage their teams to adopt similar attitudes, thereby fostering a culture of perpetual improvement. Building a lasting legacy involves more than achieving personal success; it's about creating a foundation that endures and positively impacts future generations. Effective leaders understand that their legacy is shaped by their actions, values, and the systems they put in place. By mentoring others, leaders pass on their wisdom and principles, creating a ripple effect that perpetuates their influence even after they are gone.

Mentorship is a cornerstone of personal and professional development, providing invaluable guidance, support, and encouragement. By learning from the experiences of a mentor, individuals can avoid common pitfalls and accelerate their growth. For the mentor, this relationship is an opportunity to reflect on their journey, continue learning through teaching, and reinforce their own understanding. This reciprocal process not only benefits the mentee but also strengthens the mentor's legacy, making mentorship a key strategy in building a lasting impact.

Mentorship as a Legacy-Enhancing Strategy

Mentorship is more than just a means of personal growth; it is a powerful tool for legacy building. By sharing knowledge, values, and strategies, successful individuals ensure that their influence extends beyond their own achievements. This transfer of wisdom helps shape future leaders who carry forward the principles of their mentors, contributing to sustained success and a lasting legacy. Transformational leaders, who inspire and develop others, create a ripple effect that amplifies their impact across generations.

The Mutual Benefits of Mentorship

Mentorship transcends the traditional concept of a one-way street; it is a dynamic relationship that fosters mutual growth and enrichment. While mentees benefit from the wisdom, experience, and insights of their mentors, mentors, in turn, gain access to new ideas and fresh perspectives. This exchange not only helps mentors stay attuned to emerging trends in their fields but also reignites their passion and creativity, making the relationship beneficial for both parties.

Research shows that mentorship enhances professional development and emotional well-being. According to a study by **Allen et al. (2006),** mentors often report increased job satisfaction and enhanced self-esteem from their mentoring experiences. Engaging with a mentee's enthusiasm can stimulate mentors to explore innovative solutions and rethink their own practices. This creates a learning environment that encourages experimentation and adaptation, essential traits in today's rapidly changing landscape.

Moreover, the relationship fosters accountability and reflection. As mentors guide their mentees, they are often prompted to reflect on their own career trajectories and choices. This introspection can lead to renewed focus on their goals and aspirations, thus fostering personal growth. The concept of reciprocal mentoring, where both mentor and mentee share their knowledge and skills, further exemplifies this cycle of growth. In this model, mentors may also learn valuable skills, particularly in areas like technology and social media, where younger mentees often have an edge.

This reciprocal dynamic creates a vibrant atmosphere of continuous learning, where knowledge flows in both directions. The mentoring relationship thus becomes a powerful catalyst for innovation and adaptability, ensuring that both parties remain relevant and inspired in their respective fields. Ultimately, mentorship cultivates not only professional connections but also personal growth, fostering a community of lifelong learners committed to mutual success.

Mentorship as a Social Responsibility

For many successful individuals, mentorship is viewed as a social responsibility—a way to give back to the community and uplift others. By sharing their experiences and knowledge, mentors contribute to the overall betterment of society, helping others to achieve their goals and realize their potential. This sense of responsibility drives many leaders to take on mentorship roles, ensuring that success is not just a personal achievement but a shared and perpetuated legacy. A notable example of a basketball player who embodies mentorship and social responsibility is LeBron James. Beyond his phenomenal achievements on the court, including multiple NBA championships and Most Valuable Person (MVP) awards, LeBron has made significant contributions to his community and the world at large.

LeBron founded the LeBron James Family Foundation, which focuses on education and support for children and families in need. One of his most impactful initiatives is the opening of the I PROMISE School in Akron, Ohio, designed to provide at-risk children with a comprehensive education and essential resources. This school emphasizes not only academic success but also social and emotional support, helping students overcome barriers to learning.

LeBron's influence extends beyond education; he has consistently used his platform to advocate for social justice issues, including racial equality and voting rights. His vocal stance on these matters has inspired countless individuals to engage in activism and community service.

You don't have to be a superstar to be a great mentor. A good mentor is someone who listens, teaches, and inspires others to do the same

– Michelle Obama, American Attorney

Transformational Leadership Theory, developed by **Bernard Bass(1985)**, emphasizes the role of leaders who inspire and motivate their followers to exceed their own expectations. These leaders do not just focus on the completion of tasks but actively seek to foster growth, creativity, and a sense of purpose among their team members. The transformational leader's influence goes beyond immediate performance; they cultivate an environment where individuals feel empowered to take initiative and develop their leadership skills, contributing to a legacy of excellence.

One key component of transformational leadership is the ability to provide individualized consideration. This involves mentoring and coaching followers, recognizing their unique strengths and weaknesses, and tailoring development opportunities to meet their specific needs. When leaders invest in their followers' growth, it not only enhances the followers' skills but also builds a strong bond of trust and loyalty.

Additionally, transformational leaders often serve as role models, demonstrating high ethical standards and a commitment to their vision. Their passion and dedication inspire followers to align their personal goals with the organization's objectives, creating a shared sense of purpose. This alignment fosters a higher level of engagement and satisfaction among team members, which can lead to improved performance outcomes.

The impact of transformational leadership is evident in various sectors, from corporate environments to educational institutions. For instance, research has shown that schools led by transformational leaders often see increased teacher satisfaction and student achievement **(Leithwood & Jantzi, 2000).** Similarly, organizations with transformational leaders report higher employee morale and productivity **(Judge & Piccolo, 2004).**

The story of Maria Andrejczyk., the Polish silver medalist from the 2020 Tokyo Olympics, exemplifies transformational leadership in action. Transformational leaders inspire and elevate others by transcending self-interest to prioritize the well-being of those around them. In Maria's case, her decision to auction off her Olympic silver medal to fund life-saving surgery for an 8-month-old baby in Poland demonstrates a profound act of selflessness and vision. Just as transformational leaders catalyze change and uplift communities, Maria's actions not only provided a family with hope but also mobilized collective goodwill—ultimately, the Polish supermarket chain "Zabka" purchased the medal and returned it to her, completing a cycle of compassion and leadership.

This reflects the core principles of transformational leadership, where the focus is on the moral development of both the leader and followers.

Maria's act did more than save a life—it created a ripple effect, showcasing the power of empathy, altruism, and leading by example. Such leadership transcends individual accolades and fosters a culture where humanity and ethics guide actions, much like in transformational organizations that promote well-being alongside achieving objectives.

By selflessly using her platform and achievement for the greater good, Maria displayed the hallmark of transformational leadership, inspiring others to follow in her footsteps to build a more compassionate and connected world.

Ultimately, transformational leadership not only enhances immediate performance but also cultivates a culture of leadership development, ensuring that the influence of the leader endures even after they have moved on. By inspiring others to lead and innovate, transformational leaders create a ripple effect that can significantly impact the organization's long-term success and legacy.

The greatest legacy one can pass on to one's children and grandchildren is not money or other material things accumulated in one's life, but rather a legacy of character and faith.

- Billy Graham, American Evangelist

Reciprocal Determinism, as described by Albert Bandura, highlights how personal factors, behaviors, and environmental influences continually interact and shape each other. Imagine a mentorship scenario: Sarah, an experienced marketing manager, mentors John, a new employee eager to learn about digital marketing.

Initially, Sarah provides structured guidance, sharing insights and strategies. As John implements these ideas and sees success, he grows in confidence and begins contributing fresh perspectives, suggesting innovative marketing tactics that align with current digital trends. His enthusiasm and creativity not only benefit him but also inspire Sarah, who finds herself rethinking some of her strategies and staying updated on new trends. This feedback loop exemplifies Reciprocal Determinism—John's growth and new ideas (behavior) influence Sarah (personal factor), and in turn, Sarah's expertise (environmental influence) supports John's learning. Their mutual influence creates a learning-rich environment that continually evolves, benefiting both.

Let's take an example from animal kingdom. When a baby giraffe is born, it drops roughly six feet to the ground—a harsh, startling entry into the world. Yet this fall is essential; it activates the calf's lungs, and soon after, the mother giraffe nudges her calf, encouraging it to stand up. When the calf struggles and eventually manages to get on its wobbly legs, the mother giraffe sometimes gently knocks it down again. As harsh as this may seem, it teaches the newborn the critical lesson of getting up and moving quickly, a necessary skill for survival in the wild, where predators lurk.

This example illustrates the essence of effective mentoring. A mentor, much like the mother giraffe, doesn't just protect or shield the mentee from challenges. Instead, they provide the necessary guidance and gentle pushes to help the mentee grow, learn, and become independent. Sometimes, these nudges may feel difficult or uncomfortable, but they are crucial for developing resilience, skills, and the confidence needed to navigate future challenges. A mentor ensures that while the mentee may stumble and face setbacks, they are always encouraged to rise, learn, and move forward with greater strength.

This dynamic, iterative process reflects Reciprocal Determinism in action, where the mentor-mentee relationship is a two-way street, fostering a continuous exchange that boosts growth for both.

In mentorship, the behavior of the mentor—such as providing guidance, sharing experiences, and offering feedback—can shape the mentee's development. Conversely, the mentee's responses, questions, and perspectives can influence the mentor's approach and understanding. This reciprocal relationship highlights that learning is not a one-sided process; instead, it is characterized by mutual exchange and collaboration. Jack Ma, co-founder of Alibaba, has mentored many young entrepreneurs. Through these relationships, Ma has not only imparted his business wisdom but has also gained fresh insights into new technologies and market trends from his mentees. This exchange has helped him stay innovative and relevant in a rapidly changing business environment.

The delicate balance of mentoring someone is not creating them in your own image, but giving them the opportunity to create themselves.

-Steven Spielberg, American filmmaker

Servant Leadership Theory, introduced by **Robert K. Greenleaf(1977)** essay "The Servant as Leader," reshapes traditional views of leadership by prioritizing the well-being and growth of team members over the leader's own authority or goals. Unlike top-down leadership styles, where the leader's primary focus is achieving organizational goals, servant leadership emphasizes the needs of others, empowering followers and fostering an environment where they can reach their full potential.

A servant leader actively listens, shows empathy, and focuses on building a supportive community within the organization. This leadership style centers on the belief that by serving and supporting team members, leaders can build trust and inspire loyalty, which in turn drives long-term success and sustainability. For instance, a servant leader may work closely with their team to remove obstacles, ensure resources are available, and encourage personal and professional development.

An example of servant leadership in practice is seen in companies like Southwest Airlines, where leaders empower employees to make decisions, prioritize customer satisfaction, and contribute to a positive company culture. Research shows that servant leadership can lead to higher job satisfaction, increased commitment, and a more collaborative work environment, as employees feel genuinely valued and motivated by leaders who prioritize employee's growth has inspired many organizations to focus on people-centered leadership, advocating that when leaders serve their teams, the entire organization benefits through enhanced morale, productivity, and resilience.

Mentorship beautifully embodies the essence of servant leadership, creating a unique dynamic where experienced leaders actively guide and nurture the growth of their mentees. In this relationship, mentors are not just advisors; they become trusted allies who deeply understand the aspirations and challenges faced by their mentees. This commitment to support is rooted in empathy and active listening, allowing mentors to create a safe space for exploration and self-discovery.

According to **Klamon (2007),** effective mentorship aligns seamlessly with the servant leadership model, promoting an environment where mentees feel empowered to pursue their potential without the fear of judgment. This nurturing approach fosters a culture of trust and vulnerability, enabling mentees to express their uncertainties and ambitions openly. In turn, mentors can provide tailored guidance, share valuable insights, and encourage the development of essential skills, all while prioritizing the well-being of their mentees.

The transformative power of mentorship lies in its ability to cultivate future leaders. When mentors embody the principles of servant leadership, they model behaviors that mentees can emulate, such as empathy, resilience, and a commitment to lifelong learning. For instance, a mentor who shares their own experiences of failure and growth can inspire their mentee to embrace challenges as opportunities for learning rather than obstacles to success.

The mentor's role is not merely to dispense advice but to cultivate a genuine partnership that emphasizes the mentee's growth. This approach is vital for building self-efficacy and confidence in mentees, allowing them to take on challenges and develop their skills. **Greenleaf (1977)** posits that leaders should ensure their followers feel empowered to take initiative and make decisions, ultimately leading to greater satisfaction and performance.

We make a living by what we get, but we make a life by what we give.

- Winston Churchill, UK Prime Minister [1940 A.D. to 1945 A.D.]

In the cockpit, the pilot (captain) often takes on a mentor role, guiding and supporting the co-pilot (first officer). The captain shares valuable knowledge and experience, helping the co-pilot develop essential flight skills and understand complex procedures. By delegating tasks and providing constructive feedback, the captain fosters the co-pilot's growth and confidence. The co-pilot, in turn, learns from the captain's expertise, actively seeking to apply feedback and gradually taking on more responsibilities. This mentorship relationship enhances the co-pilot's readiness for future roles and ensures effective teamwork and safety in flight operations.

Mentorship is a vital tool for perpetuating success, allowing individuals to share their knowledge, build a lasting legacy, and contribute to the growth of others. Through mentorship, successful people not only help others achieve their goals but also reinforce their own learning and remain connected to the ever-evolving landscape of their fields. By embracing the role of mentor, they ensure that their success is not just personal but also a source of inspiration and growth for future generations.

Invest in Succession Planning

Succession planning involves preparing and developing individuals to take on leadership roles in the future. It ensures that your organization or initiative continues to thrive after you step down.

What counts in life is not the mere fact that we have lived. It is what difference we have made to the lives of others that will determine the significance of the life we lead

- Nelson Mandela,

President of South Africa [1994 A.D. to 1999 A.D.]

Succession planning is a vital strategic initiative that ensures the longevity and resilience of an organization by preparing individuals to step into leadership roles. This proactive approach not only secures the future of an organization but also fosters a culture of growth and mentorship. As Nelson Mandela eloquently stated, "What counts in life is not the mere fact that we have lived. It is what difference we have made to the lives of others that will determine the significance of the life we lead." This powerful quote emphasizes the profound impact that leaders can have on future generations, reinforcing the importance of nurturing and developing successors.

Effective succession planning involves a comprehensive process that identifies and cultivates potential leaders within the organization. According to **Rothwell (2022),** organizations that prioritize succession planning are better equipped to maintain continuity and stability, particularly during transitions in leadership. By investing time and resources in developing future leaders, organizations can create a pipeline of talent that is ready to step up when needed.

This process not only ensures a seamless transition but also promotes a sense of belonging and purpose among employees. Individuals who see clear pathways for advancement are more likely to be engaged and committed to their organization. Furthermore, succession planning is an opportunity for knowledge transfer, where seasoned leaders can share their insights and experiences, empowering the next generation to navigate challenges effectively.

Research shows that organizations with robust succession plans are more likely to outperform their competitors. A study by the Center for Creative Leadership (2018) highlights that effective succession planning enhances organizational performance, employee satisfaction, and retention rates. It demonstrates that when employees feel valued and see a future within the organization, they are more inclined to contribute their best efforts.

Identifying Potential Leaders: Recognizing individuals who demonstrate leadership qualities and the potential for growth within the organization.

Providing Skills and Experience: Equipping these individuals with the necessary training and experiences to prepare them for leadership roles.

Creating a Transition Plan: Developing a structured approach to transition these individuals into leadership positions seamlessly.

These steps not only help maintain the organization's functionality but also foster a culture of leadership development.

A prime example of effective succession planning is the relationship between Steve Jobs and Tim Cook at Apple. Jobs recognized Cook's capabilities early on and strategically groomed him to be his successor. When Jobs stepped down due to health issues, Cook was prepared to take over as CEO. Under Cook's leadership, Apple has maintained its innovative edge and expanded its success, demonstrating the effectiveness of strategic succession planning **(Isaacson, 2011).**

As Peter Drucker aptly stated, "The best way to predict the future is to create it." This philosophy aligns closely with the principles of succession planning. By investing in the development of future leaders, organizations can create a robust leadership pipeline that not only predicts but shapes the future of the organization. This proactive approach ensures that leadership transitions are smooth and that the organizational vision continues to thrive.

Foster a Strong Organizational Culture

Building a strong organizational culture is like crafting the foundation of an empire that will stand the test of time. When you create an environment where people feel valued, motivated, and connected to a shared vision, the results are extraordinary. Howard Schultz, the visionary behind Starbucks, didn't just build a coffee empire—he built a community centered around respect, inclusion, and genuine customer service. Schultz once said, "The way you build a strong organization is to create a culture that people want to be a part of." This insight goes beyond catchy slogans or one-time initiatives; it's about embedding values deep into the company's DNA.

Organizational Culture Theory, proposed by **Edgar Schein (2010),** emphasizes that the collective values, beliefs, and behaviors within an organization influence how people perform, interact, and grow. Think of it as the invisible hand that guides everyday decisions. Schultz understood that in order for Starbucks to be more than just a place to get coffee, it had to stand for something meaningful—a culture where employees (referred to as "partners") felt empowered and customers felt at home.

This culture of respect and service has helped Starbucks maintain its dominance, even through turbulent times. It's what has kept customers loyal and employees motivated. In a world where businesses often chase short-term wins, Schultz demonstrated the power of investing in long-term cultural integrity. As Starbucks expanded globally, its strong culture ensured that every store—whether in Seattle or Shanghai—delivered the same welcoming experience. This not only reinforced its brand but also allowed the company to weather the storms of competition and economic downturns.

Schultz's approach also flipped the traditional corporate script: instead of seeing employees as a means to an end, Starbucks prioritized their growth and well-being. Offering benefits like healthcare and stock options even to part-time workers sent a clear message: *we value you*. This fostered loyalty, innovation, and productivity, turning a simple coffee shop into a global cultural icon.

The way you build a strong organization is to create a culture that people want to be a part of.

- Howard Schultz, CEO Starbucks

So, what can we learn from this? A strong culture doesn't just sustain a business—it creates a living legacy. When values are more than just words on a mission statement, they shape the behaviors, attitudes, and decisions of every person involved. Leaders who understand this build organizations that not only thrive but make a lasting impact on the world. Schultz didn't just create a coffee company—he sparked a movement that shows how business, when done right, can change lives.

Continuously Reflect and Adapt

Success is not a destination; it's a journey that requires continuous reflection and adaptation. Leaders who thrive in today's ever-changing world understand the power of evolution. They don't cling to old strategies or rest on past laurels. Instead, they constantly evaluate their actions, align them with their long-term vision, and adapt to new realities. This ability to reflect and adapt is not just a survival skill—it's a game-changer that ensures their legacy continues to grow and remain relevant.

Adaptive Leadership Theory, pioneered by **Heifetz (1994),** captures this essence of flexibility. It teaches leaders to thrive amid uncertainty by not only responding to change but leading it. Reflective practices allow leaders to assess what's working, what isn't, and how to pivot for greater impact. The ability to reflect, learn, and adapt separates the great from the good.

Take Jeff Bezos, for example. When Amazon began, it was a humble online bookstore. But Bezos didn't stop there. By continuously adapting Amazon's strategies, he transformed the company into the global tech and e-commerce giant we know today. Whether it was introducing cloud services through AWS, venturing into streaming, or pioneering one-click shopping, Bezos's constant reflection and willingness to evolve kept Amazon ahead of the curve. His legacy isn't just in the products he sold but in his mindset of relentless innovation.

Bezos exemplifies what leaders across industries must do: stay curious, stay humble, and never stop evolving. Those who regularly reflect on their journey and adapt to new challenges ensure their influence isn't just fleeting but builds a lasting impact. Whether you're steering a multinational corporation or leading a small team, fostering a culture of continuous learning and growth guarantees that your vision is always in tune with the times.

Building a lasting legacy requires more than just one breakthrough—it's about consistently making decisions that resonate with the future. From succession planning to fostering a resilient organizational culture, staying flexible and adaptable allows leaders to weather storms and seize opportunities that cement their mark on the world for generations to come. Just like Bezos, leaders who adapt and evolve shape the future, rather than just waiting for it to arrive.

5.2. Leaders can inspire others to not *Rest on their Laurels*

Leaders can inspire others to not rest on their laurels by modeling a commitment to continuous improvement, embracing challenges, and fostering a culture of growth and innovation. Leaders who actively pursue their own growth and development set a powerful example. By continually seeking new knowledge, skills, and challenges, they demonstrate that excellence is a journey, not a destination. Their dedication to personal and professional development encourages others to adopt a similar mindset.

Demonstrating a Commitment to Continuous Learning

Leaders who prioritize lifelong learning set a dynamic example for their teams and followers, demonstrating that leadership is an evolving journey rather than a static position. According to Adult Learning Theory **(Knowles, 1980),** adults are intrinsically motivated to learn when the content is relevant to their lives or careers. By embracing continuous learning, leaders convey that growth is vital at every stage of life and career. This mindset cultivates an organizational culture where curiosity and innovation thrive, ultimately enhancing performance and adaptability.

A prime example of this principle from the world of sports is Andre Agassi, the iconic tennis player of the 1990s. Known for his extraordinary talent and fierce competitiveness, Agassi also exemplified a commitment to continuous learning and personal growth. Throughout his career, Agassi faced numerous challenges, including struggles with motivation and injuries. Rather than succumbing to these obstacles, he sought knowledge and self-improvement, both on and off the court.

Agassi's dedication to learning was evident in his pursuit of new techniques and strategies, which he often incorporated into his game. He sought out coaches who could provide fresh insights, and he was open to adapting his style to enhance his performance. Moreover, Agassi's autobiography, *Open*, reveals his introspective nature and desire to understand not just the mechanics of tennis but also the psychological aspects of the game. He often reflected on his experiences and emotions, allowing him to grow as both an athlete and a person.

His relentless pursuit of knowledge and self-improvement not only contributed to his success—winning eight Grand Slam titles—but also inspired a generation of athletes to approach their careers with a similar mindset. Agassi's story illustrates that when leaders commit to learning and growth, they inspire their teams to think bigger, take risks, and challenge the status quo.

A similar example is George Lucas, the creator of *Star Wars*, who revolutionized filmmaking by constantly learning new techniques and experimenting with technology. Lucas pioneered computer-generated imagery (CGI) and digital filmmaking, setting the stage for the future of cinema. His commitment to mastering new methods and innovating beyond traditional practices didn't just lead to the success of *Star Wars* but transformed the film industry itself. Lucas's curiosity and forward-thinking approach reflect the idea that, to shape the future, leaders must be proactive learners and inventors of new realities.

In both cases, these leaders didn't just wait for the future to happen—they actively created it. Leaders who embrace this mindset, continually educating themselves and seeking new skills, ensure that their influence not only drives their own success but also shapes the trajectory of their industries and inspires those around them to strive for more.

Embracing Failure and Resilience

Leaders who openly embrace their failures and turn them into valuable learning moments create a vibrant atmosphere of resilience and innovation within their teams. This kind of vulnerability doesn't signify weakness; rather, it showcases a profound strength that can inspire others. In a world where success stories dominate social media feeds, it's easy to forget the missteps and failures that often lead to those triumphs.

When leaders openly acknowledge their stumbles, they send a powerful message: failure is not a dead end but a vital part of the journey toward mastery. Consider the legendary coach Phil Jackson, who guided the Chicago Bulls and the Los Angeles Lakers to multiple championships. Jackson often reflected on his own coaching failures, emphasizing how they taught him critical lessons about team dynamics and resilience. His willingness to share these insights allowed his players to understand that even the most successful leaders face setbacks.

Additionally, when leaders share their recovery strategies—how they picked themselves up, learned from their experiences, and moved forward—they normalize the conversation around failure. This transparency fosters an environment where team members feel safe to take risks and innovate, knowing that mistakes are part of the growth process.

Brené Brown, an expert on vulnerability and leadership, in her book *Dare to Lead* emphasizes the idea that being a great leader isn't about projecting an image of perfection. Instead, it's about being open to showing flaws and learning from them. Her research shows that when leaders are honest about their imperfections, they create an atmosphere of trust and psychological safety within their teams. People feel more comfortable sharing ideas, being creative, and taking risks, all without the fear of being judged or criticized harshly.

Brown explains that vulnerability is not a weakness; rather, it's a mark of courage. When leaders openly admit they don't have all the answers or share stories of their own failures, it makes them more relatable and approachable. This behavior demonstrates that it's okay to be imperfect and that growth comes from learning through experience. It also sets a powerful example, encouraging others to be authentic and innovative, knowing that mistakes are a natural part of the process.

In this way, Brown's approach to leadership transforms how teams operate. Leaders who embrace vulnerability not only strengthen connections but also drive greater collaboration and engagement, helping their organizations thrive.

In essence, the key to transforming failure into a stepping stone lies in how leaders bounce back. By showcasing resilience and a commitment to learning, they not only enhance their own leadership but also empower their teams to strive for excellence. In doing so, they cultivate a culture where innovation thrives, and challenges are viewed as opportunities rather than obstacles.

Embracing failure as a teacher can revolutionize how teams operate, driving them toward unprecedented success. So, the next time you face a setback, remember: it's not just about falling; it's about how you rise again and inspire others to do the same!

Growth Mindset Theory by **Dweck (2006)** underscores that individuals who see challenges as growth opportunities outperform those who view them as threats. Leaders who adopt and model this mindset help their teams realize that failure is not a signal to give up but rather an invitation to grow stronger, smarter, and more adaptable. They cultivate an environment where employees are not afraid to take calculated risks, knowing that even if they fail, they'll emerge better equipped for the next challenge.

Phil Knight, co-founder of Nike, exemplifies the philosophy of learning from failure. In the early years of Nike, Knight faced numerous challenges, including financial struggles and skepticism from investors and retailers. One of his biggest setbacks was his initial failure to secure a distribution deal with major retailers, which threatened the company's survival. However, Knight's resilience and ability to learn from these obstacles were crucial to Nike's eventual success. He reframed each setback as an opportunity for growth and innovation, ultimately transforming Nike into a global brand. Knight's story demonstrates that failure is not the end, but a necessary step on the path to success. His mindset encourages others to embrace challenges and keep pushing forward with determination

One of the most powerful reminders of this approach comes from Winston Churchill's famous words: "Success is not final, failure is not fatal: It is the courage to continue that counts." Leaders who live by this credo inspire their teams to keep pushing forward, to embrace failures as part of the process, and to understand that growth and innovation often come from the ashes of setbacks.

It's this ability to pick up the pieces, adapt, and keep going that separates the great leaders from the rest. The best leaders ignite that same fire in their teams, ensuring that the fear of failure never quashes the potential for greatness. In a world obsessed with instant success, those who understand the power of perseverance will always have the upper hand.

Setting and Pursuing Ambitious Goals

Leaders who set and pursue ambitious goals exemplify a relentless commitment to high standards and continuous improvement, driving their teams to strive for excellence and to continually push beyond their limits. This principle is rooted in Goal-Setting Theory by **Locke & Latham (2002)**, which asserts that specific and challenging goals lead to higher performance than vague or easily attainable ones. A perfect illustration of this is Dwayne "The Rock" Johnson, a figure who embodies ambition at every turn.

From his early days as a professional wrestler, where he set the ambitious goal of becoming the top star in the WWE, to his meteoric rise as a Hollywood powerhouse and entrepreneur, Johnson's journey is marked by a series of challenging objectives. His mantra, "Success is not about greatness. It's about consistency. Consistent hard work gains success. Greatness will come," reflects his belief that sustained effort, rather than fleeting moments of brilliance, is the true driver of achievement. This perspective not only defines his personal journey but also serves as a beacon of inspiration for countless fans and aspiring leaders worldwide.

Johnson's strategic goal-setting extends beyond his personal career; it shapes his approach to teamwork and leadership. He emphasizes the importance of consistent effort and resilience, encouraging his team to adopt a mindset where every small victory contributes to larger success. For example, in his production company, Seven Bucks Productions, he sets ambitious project goals that challenge his team to innovate and deliver quality content, from blockbuster films to television shows.

Moreover, Johnson's commitment to his fitness regime serves as another testament to this principle. He famously shares his intense workout routines and nutrition plans, underscoring that the road to physical greatness is paved with daily consistency and effort. This not only inspires his fans but also reinforces his brand as one that values hard work and resilience.

In today's fast-paced world, where instant success can often overshadow the value of perseverance, Johnson's story reminds us that the true essence of success lies in setting ambitious goals, remaining consistent, and nurturing a culture of hard work and accountability within teams. By modeling these behaviors, leaders can inspire others to embrace a growth mindset and pursue excellence, ultimately leading to greater collective achievements.

Demonstrating Work Ethic and Integrity

Leaders who embody a strong work ethic and unwavering integrity not only inspire their teams but also set the tone for the entire organization. By demonstrating dedication, honesty, and ethical behavior, they foster a culture of trust and excellence that permeates every level of the organization. This aligns perfectly with Servant Leadership Theory **Greenleaf (2007),** which emphasizes that leaders who prioritize serving their teams and leading with integrity cultivate a supportive and ethical work environment. Such leaders create a ripple effect, encouraging their employees to mirror these values in their daily interactions and decisions.

Satya Nadella, CEO of Microsoft, stands as a prime example of a leader who exemplifies these principles. Since taking the helm, Nadella has transformed Microsoft's culture by emphasizing empathy, integrity, and a relentless work ethic. He has famously stated, *"Our industry does not respect tradition—it only respects innovation."* This mindset has fueled a renewed focus on collaboration and ethical behavior, enhancing not only the company's internal dynamics but also its reputation in the marketplace.

Under Nadella's leadership, Microsoft has experienced a renaissance, shifting from a competitive, cutthroat environment to one that prioritizes learning and inclusivity. This shift is evident in initiatives like the "Growth Mindset" philosophy, which encourages employees to embrace challenges, learn from feedback, and persevere through obstacles. As a result, Microsoft has not only regained its status as a tech giant but has also become a beacon of corporate responsibility and innovation.

Moreover, Nadella's emphasis on integrity is reflected in Microsoft's commitment to ethical AI practices and transparency in business operations. By prioritizing ethical considerations in technology development, he has set a standard that many companies now aspire to achieve. This approach not only enhances Microsoft's brand but also builds a loyal customer base that trusts the company's mission and values.

The function of leadership is to produce more leaders, not more followers.

- Ralph Nader, American Political Activist.

Nadella's leadership serves as a refreshing reminder of the power of integrity and a strong work ethic. Leaders who emulate his approach can create a legacy of trust, collaboration, and excellence that benefits not only their teams but also the broader community.

Encouraging Innovation and Creativity

Leaders who actively promote innovation and creativity set an example for their teams by valuing and rewarding new ideas. This approach fosters an environment where creativity is encouraged and celebrated.

Innovation Leadership Theory by **Kanter (1983)** suggests that leaders who support and nurture innovation create environments where new ideas can flourish. By encouraging creativity and experimentation, leaders inspire their teams to contribute innovative solutions.

One notable leader in the Indian startup ecosystem is Vijay Shekhar Sharma, the founder of **Paytm**. Under Sharma's leadership, Paytm has revolutionized digital payments in India, particularly after the demonetization initiative in 2016. His commitment to exploring new avenues for growth while exploiting the existing digital payment framework has been a game changer for millions of consumers and businesses across the country.

Sharma's innovative approach has not only expanded Paytm's offerings beyond payments to include financial services, e-commerce, and even insurance but has also fostered a culture of rapid experimentation within the organization. By prioritizing customer feedback and staying agile, Paytm has managed to adapt its services to meet the evolving needs of its user base. This strategy aligns well with the concept of "explore and exploit," as Sharma continuously seeks new opportunities while optimizing existing ones.

Moreover, Sharma has focused on building a strong brand identity that resonates with the youth, emphasizing user-friendly technology and customer-centric solutions. His leadership style encourages his team to think creatively and take calculated risks, further driving innovation within the company.

Innovation distinguishes between a leader and a follower - Steve Jobs

Leading by example is a powerful way to inspire others to avoid complacency and continuously strive for excellence. By demonstrating a commitment to learning, embracing resilience, setting ambitious goals, maintaining a strong work ethic, and encouraging innovation, leaders can create a culture of growth and achievement. These strategies not only enhance personal and organizational success but also leave a lasting legacy that influences future generations.

5.3. Creating a Culture of Perpetual Growth

Creating a culture of perpetual growth is like planting a garden where seeds of learning and innovation are constantly nurtured. This environment cultivates resilience, curiosity, and adaptability, allowing individuals and organizations to thrive in a fast-paced world. It's a mindset that goes beyond the traditional view of success as a finish line; instead, it treats each achievement as a stepping stone towards greater challenges and opportunities.

At the heart of this culture lies the belief that feedback is a gift. Organizations that prioritize open communication and collaboration empower their teams to embrace constructive criticism and learn from both successes and setbacks. This encourages a collective drive towards improvement, where everyone feels valued and motivated to contribute ideas. Stretch goals become a norm, pushing individuals out of their comfort zones and sparking creativity.

Moreover, organizations that foster perpetual growth prioritize continuous learning and professional development. They offer regular training sessions, mentorship programs, and skill enhancement workshops, creating pathways for employees to expand their knowledge and expertise. This commitment to personal development not only boosts employee morale but also enhances overall organizational performance.

In this dynamic environment, complacency is the enemy. Individuals are empowered to challenge themselves continuously, leveraging new knowledge and technologies to innovate and adapt. This proactive attitude not only ensures long-term success but also keeps organizations relevant and competitive in an ever-evolving landscape.

The benefits of a perpetual growth culture are manifold. It leads to a workforce that is engaged, resilient, and equipped to tackle the uncertainties of the future. By fostering such an environment, organizations can cultivate a thriving ecosystem that consistently pushes the boundaries of what they can achieve, ensuring a legacy of innovation and excellence.

EXERCISE

1. Mentorship Mapping Exercise: Identify potential mentors and mentees within your network.

Instructions:

- Create a visual map or chart listing individuals you admire or who have influenced you in your field.
- For each person, note how they could serve as a mentor (skills, knowledge) and whom you could mentor in return.
- Reflect on specific lessons you hope to learn from them and how you can provide guidance to others.

2. Legacy Vision Board: Clarify what legacy you want to leave behind.

Instructions:

- Gather materials like magazines, scissors, glue, and a board.
- Cut out images, words, or phrases that resonate with your vision of success and legacy.
- Arrange them on the board to create a visual representation of your aspirations and the impact you wish to have.
- Display this board in a prominent place as a daily reminder of your goals.

3. Growth Mindset Reflection Journal: Cultivate a growth mindset by reflecting on your experiences.

- Dedicate a journal for this exercise. At the end of each week, write about a challenge you faced and how you approached it.
- Reflect on what you learned from the experience and how it contributes to your growth.
- Include examples of how you can apply these lessons in the future to inspire others.

4. Team Growth Challenge: Foster a culture of perpetual growth within your team or organization.

Instructions:

- Organize a "Growth Challenge" within your team. Set a specific goal (e.g., learn a new skill, complete a project outside of comfort zones) over a defined period.
- Encourage team members to share their progress and learnings regularly in team meetings.
- Celebrate successes and encourage open discussions about failures and lessons learned.

5. Inspirational Leadership Discussion Group: Inspire ongoing development and mentorship among peers.

Instructions:

- Form a small group of like-minded individuals who are interested in leadership and personal development.

- Meet bi-weekly to discuss influential leadership books, articles, or podcasts.
- Share personal insights and challenges, encouraging each other to set actionable goals for personal and professional growth.

Chapter 6: Evolving with Purpose: The Art of Periodic Self-Reinvention

6.1. The Need for Rejuvenate

In a fast-paced world where technology and market demands are in constant flux, the ability to reinvent oneself isn't just a competitive advantage—it's essential for survival. Reinvention is about adapting to change, seizing new opportunities, and staying relevant. Whether it's personal growth or career evolution, those who embrace the process of periodic reinvention can thrive, while those who resist often face stagnation.

Consider the story of *Narayana Murthy*, the founder of Infosys, one of India's most successful IT services companies. Murthy's journey is a testament to reinvention. Starting Infosys in 1981, Murthy faced challenges from a tech industry that was undergoing massive shifts with globalization and technological advancements. Rather than sticking to traditional IT services, he constantly adapted the company's strategies—shifting to global markets, embracing outsourcing, and fostering innovation to cater to international demand. This adaptability allowed Infosys to rise as a global leader.

Murthy's philosophy was driven by the need to stay ahead of the curve. By continuously questioning the status quo and updating the company's direction, he transformed Infosys into a global powerhouse, employing thousands and inspiring countless entrepreneurs. In contrast, companies that failed to reinvent—like Nokia, which was slow to adapt to the smartphone era—saw rapid declines.

The greatest danger in times of turbulence is not the turbulence—it is to act with yesterday's logic - Peter Drucker, Educator & Consultant

The lesson is clear: whether you're an individual or an organization, reinvention is the key to staying relevant in a constantly changing world. The Theory of Adaptive Change, as proposed by John Kotter, highlights this necessity, emphasizing that those who embrace change thrive, while those who resist it are left behind.

6.2. Embracing New Skills and Knowledge

Reinvention is more than just a change in direction—it's an ongoing process of learning and acquiring new skills to stay competitive in an ever-evolving world. Lifelong learning is at the core of this process, as it enables individuals to remain adaptable, continuously improving their abilities and perspectives to meet new challenges head-on. This idea is grounded in the *Lifelong Learning Theory* given by **Knowles (1975),** which emphasizes that growth and education should not cease after formal schooling. Instead, it's a lifelong endeavor that helps people evolve in line with changing environments.

Anyone who stops learning is old, whether at twenty or eighty. Anyone who keeps learning stays young. The greatest thing in life is to keep your mind young.

-   Henry Ford, American Industrialist

A notable example of lifelong learning and reinvention is Muhammad Yunus, the founder of Grameen Bank and Nobel Peace Prize laureate. Yunus' journey is a testament to how continuous learning and adaptation can lead to transformative social change. Originally an economics professor, Yunus' was deeply moved by the poverty he witnessed in Bangladesh. He started experimenting with microcredit, providing small loans to impoverished people, particularly women, to help them start businesses and improve their livelihoods.

Instead of buying your children all the things you never had, you should teach them all the things you were never taught. Material wears out, but knowledge stays.

-Bruce Lee, Hong Kong-American Martial Artist and Actor

Yunus' innovative approach to finance and his willingness to learn from his experiences led to the creation of Grameen Bank, a model that has been replicated around the world. Despite facing numerous challenges and skepticism, Yunus continued to adapt and refine his model, embracing new strategies to ensure the success and sustainability of his work. His example highlights the power of lifelong learning in shaping a vision that not only changes lives but also challenges conventional norms in finance and poverty alleviation.

6.3. Adapting to New Roles and Environments

Reinvention often requires adapting to new roles or environments. This might involve changing industries, pursuing new career paths, or adjusting to different life circumstances.

Role Theory suggests that individuals navigate different social roles throughout their lives. Successful reinvention involves effectively transitioning between roles and adapting to new expectations and responsibilities **Biddle (1986).**

An eagle typically has a lifespan of 60 to 70 years. However, when it reaches the age of 40, the eagle faces a critical point in its life. Its long talons become weak and no longer effective for catching prey. Its sharp beak becomes bent, and its feathers become thick and heavy, making it difficult to fly. Faced with these challenges, the eagle must make a tough decision: it can either continue its life in this deteriorated state or go through a painful process of renewal.

If the eagle chooses renewal, it flies to a high mountain and perches on a rock. There, it goes through a 150-day process of transformation. First, it knocks its beak against the rock until it falls off, allowing a new, stronger beak to grow back. Once the beak has regrown, the eagle plucks out its old talons, and when the new talons grow in, it begins plucking out its heavy, worn-out feathers. After five months of pain and struggle, the eagle emerges renewed, with a fresh set of feathers, talons, and a sharp beak. It is then able to live for another 30 years, hunting and flying as it did in its youth. The story of the eagle's renewal is a powerful metaphor for change and adaptability. It teaches us that sometimes we need to let go of old habits, beliefs, or situations that are holding us back. The process may be painful and challenging, but it's necessary for growth and continued success. Just like the eagle, we must be willing to embrace change and endure temporary discomfort to emerge stronger, renewed, and more capable of facing life's challenges.

The only way to make sense out of change is to plunge into it, move with it, and join the dance

- Alan Watts, Writer and Speaker

Though this story is a metaphor rather than a biological fact, it is often used to inspire people to take on transformation and self-reinvention when they reach difficult crossroads in life.

6.4. Leveraging Personal Strengths and Passions

Successful reinvention isn't just about change; it's about aligning with personal passions and leveraging strengths to create new paths that lead to growth and fulfillment. The *Self-Determination Theory* **Deci & Ryan (1985)** suggests that motivation and well-being are significantly heightened when individuals engage in activities driven by intrinsic interests. In other words, when we tap into what we truly love and where we excel, we can unleash tremendous potential for success and personal satisfaction.

An intriguing example of this concept is Japanese entrepreneur Masayoshi Son, the founder and CEO of SoftBank. Son's journey is a story of reinvention fueled by his passion for technology and innovation. Born in a modest family in Japan, Son initially took a bold step by moving to the U.S. to study at the University of California, Berkeley. He didn't shy away from risk—during his studies, he built a successful business selling translation devices. But that was only the beginning. After returning to Japan, Son saw the future of technology and founded SoftBank, turning it into a tech investment powerhouse.

Son's reinvention came when he placed a seemingly reckless bet on Alibaba in its early days—an investment that many questioned. But this audacious move paid off massively, making SoftBank one of the biggest players in global tech. Son's journey reflects not just personal reinvention but also the ability to see potential where others might see risk. He aligned his ventures with his love for technology, investing in everything from telecommunications to cutting-edge AI.

The twist in Son's story came when he nearly lost it all during the dot-com bubble burst, a time when SoftBank's stock plummeted. But instead of retreating, Son leaned into his passion, doubling down on his belief in the future of technology. His unwavering commitment to his vision turned the tables, and today, SoftBank is synonymous with innovation and the future of tech.

The only limit to our realization of tomorrow is our doubts of today

- Franklin D. Roosevelt, US President

By aligning his work with his strengths and passions, Son exemplifies how personal reinvention, when done strategically, can lead not just to success but to industry-shaping influence. His story reminds us that reinvention isn't about running away from failure—it's about learning from it and coming back stronger.

6.5. Overcoming Fear and Resistance

Reinvention is a powerful, transformative process that often forces individuals to confront deeply rooted fears and the inevitable resistance to change. The **Change Curve model**, originally inspired by Elisabeth Kübler-Ross's work on grief, captures the psychological journey people undergo during significant transitions. It vividly outlines the four main emotional stages: denial, resistance, exploration, and commitment.

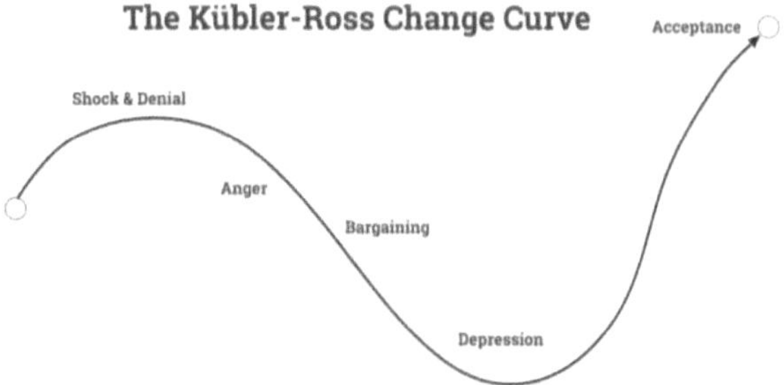

Change Curve Model

A compelling example of resilience and reinvention comes from **Ralph Lauren**, the renowned fashion designer, who grew up in a poor neighborhood in the Bronx, New York. Raised in a working-class family, Lauren was the son of Jewish immigrants and had a modest upbringing. He attended college for a brief period but dropped out and enlisted in the U.S. Army. After serving, he worked as a salesman for Brooks Brothers, where he sold ties, and it was during this time that he became inspired to design his own line of neckties.

Despite not having formal fashion education or any connections in the industry, Ralph Lauren faced a steep uphill battle. His first collection was met with skepticism, as many doubted a self-taught designer could succeed in the highly competitive fashion world. He received numerous rejections, but he didn't give up. Lauren continued to refine his designs, eventually launching the Polo Ralph Lauren brand in 1967.

His journey through setbacks and rejections is a clear example of the **Change Curve**. Lauren experienced initial denial—his ideas were not taken seriously by the established fashion world. He encountered resistance from critics who doubted his skills and vision. But instead of giving in to the fear of failure, he embraced the challenges, adjusted his approach, and persevered. As Polo Ralph Lauren grew, his brand revolutionized the fashion industry, turning casual wear into a symbol of luxury and style.

The greatest glory in living lies not in never falling, but in rising every time we fall.

- Nelson Mandela,
President of South Africa [1994 A.D. to 1999 A.D.]

Ralph Lauren's story exemplifies how someone from an unconventional background can reinvent themselves by embracing resilience, believing in their vision, and persevering through adversity. His success is a powerful testament to how resilience can turn seemingly insurmountable obstacles into stepping stones toward achieving greatness.

6.6. Setting Goals and Tracking Progress

Reinvention is a vital aspect of personal and professional growth. By embracing new skills, adapting to new roles, leveraging personal strengths, and overcoming resistance, individuals can navigate change effectively and achieve long-term success. Periodic reinvention ensures that you remain relevant, fulfilled, and prepared for the future, turning challenges into opportunities for growth. Effective reinvention demands clear goal-setting and regular progress tracking, ensuring that efforts remain aligned with desired outcomes. The *SMART Goals Framework* (Specific, Measurable, Achievable, Relevant, Time-bound) provides an essential structure for creating clarity, focus, and actionable plans. By breaking down the reinvention process into measurable milestones, individuals can monitor their journey, make necessary adjustments, and ultimately stay on course toward achieving their vision.

A compelling example of this strategy is Phumzile Mlambo-Ngcuka, the former Deputy President of South Africa and a prominent advocate for women's rights and social justice. Throughout her career, Mlambo-Ngcuka has demonstrated the power of setting clear goals and tracking progress to achieve meaningful change. During her tenure as Executive Director of UN Women, she prioritized specific objectives aimed at promoting gender equality and women's empowerment on a global scale. Mlambo-Ngcuka established measurable targets related to women's economic empowerment, political participation, and access to education, ensuring that her efforts were both ambitious and achievable.

By focusing on SMART goals, Mlambo-Ngcuka was able to mobilize resources, engage stakeholders, and drive initiatives that resulted in significant progress in advancing women's rights. For instance, her efforts to promote the *HeForShe* campaign engaged men and boys as advocates for gender equality, demonstrating the effectiveness of a structured goal-oriented approach.

You don't learn to walk by following rules. You learn by doing, and by falling over.

- Richard Branson, CEO, Virgin Group

Mlambo-Ngcuka's disciplined tracking of progress enabled her to adapt strategies as needed, ensuring that the initiatives she led remained relevant and impactful in an ever-evolving global landscape. This method of setting clear, actionable goals and systematically assessing their outcomes exemplifies how a goal-oriented mindset can lead to successful reinvention, both personally and within organizations.

6.7. Dismantle yourself

Reinventing oneself as an actor involves a dynamic and often transformative journey of self-discovery and adaptation, where performers constantly evolve to stay relevant and captivating. This reinvention begins with a candid self-assessment—actors look inward, evaluating their previous performances, identifying their strengths, and pinpointing areas for growth. Just as seasoned craftsmen refine their tools, actors sharpen their skills, acknowledging past successes but also recognizing where they've played it safe or fallen short.

To truly reinvent, actors must break free from their established mold. This often means stepping into unfamiliar territory, exploring roles that challenge their typecast image, or diving into genres that push their boundaries. For instance, an actor known for comedic roles might take on a serious drama or action-packed thriller, forcing themselves to develop new emotional and physical responses. Reinvention doesn't just happen on the surface—it requires a deep commitment to craft. Actors might undergo rigorous physical transformations, engage in voice coaching, or even learn entirely new languages to fully embody characters that demand something extraordinary.

This constant reinvention is necessary in an industry that never stops evolving. New trends, societal shifts, and audience preferences emerge, and those who fail to adapt risk becoming irrelevant. Consider the example of Hollywood legends like Robert De Niro or Meryl Streep, who have maintained long, flourishing careers by embracing a variety of roles, from the heart-wrenching to the absurd. They continuously mirror the pulse of societal change by taking on roles that speak to contemporary issues.

The magic of reinvention lies in its capacity to mesmerize—viewers love seeing actors defy expectations and present fresh, previously unseen aspects of themselves. It's not just a matter of changing appearance or adopting a new style; it's about diving deep into the human condition and revealing unexplored layers of their personas, keeping audiences emotionally invested. Through this process, actors breathe life into their characters in ways that are both timeless and utterly relevant.

In sum, the dismantling and reinvention of an actor's persona is like peeling back layers of an onion, revealing something new with every transformation. This journey requires resilience, curiosity, and the audacity to embrace discomfort, but it is what keeps performances fresh, exciting, and, most importantly, unforgettable.

6.8. Steps to Personal Reinvention

Personal reinvention often requires a deep reflection and a willingness to challenge one's current state to pave the way for a new, more fulfilling path. A compelling example of personal reinvention is Melanie Perkins, the co-founder and CEO of Canva. Her journey illustrates the power of self-assessment and determination in driving innovation and success.

Step 1: Self-Assessment and Reflection: Conduct a Personal Audit

Melanie Perkins started her entrepreneurial journey while she was still a student at the University of Western Australia. She noticed that many of her peers struggled with using design software, which was often complex and intimidating. This realization prompted her to reflect on her own experiences and skills, identifying a gap in the market for an easier, more accessible design tool.

Rather than simply accepting the existing limitations of design software, Perkins embraced her vision for a user-friendly platform that anyone could use, regardless of their design background. However, her initial attempts to launch Canva faced challenges. In her first business venture, she created a company that offered online tools for designing school yearbooks. Though the idea was promising, it highlighted the need for a more robust platform that could cater to a wider audience.

After securing initial funding and feedback, Perkins continued to refine her concept. She and her co-founder, Cliff Obrecht, moved to Silicon Valley to gain access to a broader network and resources. This phase of her journey involved reassessing their goals, identifying what was essential for their success, and honing their approach.

When you live for strong purpose, hardwork is not option it is necessity.

– Steve Pavlina, Motivational Speaker.

Ultimately, Perkins transformed her vision into reality with Canva, which launched in 2013. Today, Canva is valued at billions of dollars and serves millions of users globally. Her journey showcases the importance of continuous reflection, adaptability, and the courage to pursue one's passions.

In *Harry Potter*, the phrase *"the wand chooses the wizard"* captures a magical truth: a wizard doesn't choose their wand; instead, the wand finds the wizard it best matches. This concept goes beyond magic—it's a powerful metaphor for how life works. Often, the roles, opportunities, or paths that shape us are not the ones we actively chase but those that align with our true nature. Just as Harry's wand connected with his unique qualities, life has a way of presenting us with opportunities that resonate with our strengths and potential.

However, recognizing and accepting what "chooses" us requires self-awareness. In life, the equivalent of the wand might be a career, a passion, or a calling that feels natural and fulfilling. Sometimes, people miss these signs because they are too focused on following what others expect or chasing what looks appealing but doesn't truly fit. This is where the real lesson lies: ***don't rest on your laurels*** or cling to the familiar. Instead, trust the process and stay open to what life offers.

When you embrace what truly resonates with you, you unlock your best potential. Just as the right wand helps a wizard perform great magic, finding and accepting what aligns with your abilities and passions allows you to achieve your best performance. The magic lies in letting yourself be chosen by the right opportunities and giving your best to grow with them.

Step 2. Set Clear Goals: Define Your Vision and Objectives

Setting clear, actionable goals is a crucial step for anyone looking to reinvent themselves. This process not only clarifies your vision but also serves as a roadmap for achieving your aspirations. By utilizing the SMART criteria—Specific, Measurable, Achievable, Relevant, and

Time-bound—you can create structured goals that effectively guide your reinvention journey.

Consider the personal journey of Japanese author and marathon runner Haruki Murakami. Murakami had a successful career running a jazz club in Tokyo but decided in his thirties to pursue writing. Driven by a passion for storytelling, he set a specific goal: to write a full-length novel. Murakami knew that to become a successful writer, he needed to develop the discipline and skills required to produce high-quality work consistently.

He made his progress measurable by committing to writing a certain number of pages every day, holding himself accountable to this target. Realistic goals were also a priority. Murakami understood that becoming a literary success wouldn't happen overnight. He gave himself years to refine his craft, enter competitions, and publish his books, gradually building his reputation.

Murakami's goal of becoming a novelist was relevant to his inner passion and vision for his life, making the journey fulfilling even when he faced challenges. He also ensured his goals were time-bound. He set personal deadlines for writing drafts, getting feedback, and revising his manuscripts. This disciplined approach to goal setting allowed Murakami to transition successfully from running a business to becoming a world-renowned author.

Haruki Murakami's reinvention story illustrates the power of structured goal-setting. By following the SMART framework, he turned his aspirations into tangible achievements, reminding us all those clear goals are the first step toward profound personal transformation.

***Step 3. Acquire New Skills and Knowledge: Embrace Lifelong
Learning***

Acquiring new skills and knowledge is vital in today's fast-paced world,
and embracing lifelong learning is the key to staying relevant and
competitive. Emma Watson, a renowned actress and activist, exemplifies
this journey of continuous growth. Despite her fame from playing
Hermione Granger in the *Harry Potter* series, Watson didn't rest on her
laurels; instead, she pursued an education at Brown University,
graduating with a degree in English literature in 2014. Her dedication to
education reflects the principles of the Theory of Lifelong Learning,
which underscores the importance of ongoing personal and professional
development **Knowles (1975).**

Watson's journey extends beyond academia; she has also engaged in
various initiatives promoting gender equality, such as her role as a UN
Women Goodwill Ambassador. In her speeches and public appearances,
she emphasizes the need for education and empowerment, proving that
learning is not limited to traditional settings. She actively promotes the
idea that acquiring new knowledge—whether through formal education,
workshops, or personal projects—can lead to meaningful change.

*Education is the most powerful weapon which you can use to change the
world*

- Nelson Mandela,

President of South Africa [1994 A.D. to 1999 A.D.]

Moreover, Watson has taken on diverse roles in films that challenge her
range as an actress. For instance, her performance in *Beauty and the*

Beast required her to develop singing skills, which she embraced wholeheartedly. This willingness to step outside her comfort zone and learn new skills showcases her commitment to lifelong learning, allowing her to evolve not only as an actress but also as a person.

The Theory of Lifelong Learning emphasizes the importance of ongoing education and skill development for personal and professional growth **Knowles (1975).**

By continually expanding her horizons, Watson inspires others to recognize that the pursuit of knowledge is a lifelong journey. In an era where adaptability is crucial, her story highlights the power of embracing lifelong learning to foster personal growth, resilience, and the ability to make a significant impact in the world.

Step 4. Experiment and Take Risks: Embrace Experimentation

Embracing experimentation and taking risks can be transformative in the journey of reinvention, and one compelling example from Russia is Pavel Durov, the founder of the popular messaging app Telegram. Initially known as the creator of VKontakte (VK), Russia's largest social network, Durov's path to success was paved with bold moves and calculated risks that ultimately led him to innovate in the realm of digital communication.

In 2014, Durov made the daring decision to leave VK, a company he built from the ground up. Instead of retreating, he embraced the challenge and ventured into the uncharted territory of creating Telegram. His vision was to develop a messaging platform that prioritized user privacy and freedom of speech, areas often neglected in many social media platforms. This leap into a new industry not only showcased his commitment to innovation but also his belief in the importance of experimentation.

The Innovation Adoption Curve, developed by sociologist Everett Rogers, outlines how new technologies or ideas are adopted in a society, ranging from innovators and early adopters to the early majority, late majority, and laggards.

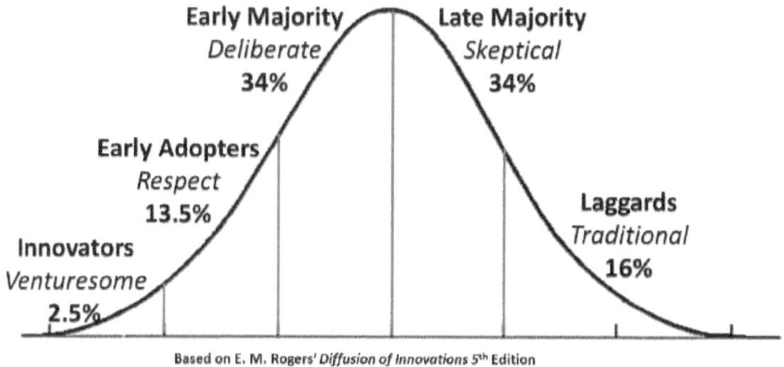

Based on E. M. Rogers' *Diffusion of Innovations* 5th Edition

Pavel Durov's journey with Telegram exemplifies this curve in action. When Durov launched Telegram in 2013, the messaging app market was already saturated with established giants like WhatsApp and Facebook Messenger. Entering this competitive space required a bold approach that appealed to the innovators and early adopters—those who are willing to try new technology that offers unique advantages. Telegram's focus on privacy, security, and cutting-edge features attracted this audience swiftly. With offerings like end-to-end encryption, self-destructing messages, and large broadcasting channels, Telegram differentiated itself by emphasizing values that mattered deeply to its target users.

By prioritizing these features, Telegram gained momentum, eventually crossing over to attract a broader audience. The app's ability to continuously adapt and innovate—such as introducing Bots, Groups with massive member capacities, and the integration of a rich media ecosystem—fueled its exponential growth. As Durov embraced a philosophy of constant experimentation, Telegram evolved into a global communications powerhouse, particularly resonating with users who were concerned about data privacy and state surveillance.

This strategy was instrumental in Telegram surpassing 700 million users as of 2021, illustrating how a keen understanding of the Innovation Adoption Curve can enable a new product to disrupt even the most crowded markets. By leveraging unique value propositions and appealing to early adopters, Durov set Telegram apart and ensured its place in the digital landscape as a revolutionary communication tool.

You miss 100% of the shots you don't take

- Wayne Gretzky, Former ice hockey player

Durov's story is a testament to the power of experimentation and risk-taking. By stepping outside his comfort zone and challenging the status quo, he not only reinvented his career but also transformed the way people communicate in an increasingly digital world.

Step 5. Seek Feedback and Mentorship: Leverage External Perspectives

Seeking feedback and mentorship plays a pivotal role in the process of reinvention. When embarking on a journey of change or transformation, external perspectives can act as a mirror that reflects strengths, weaknesses, and opportunities that may otherwise go unnoticed. Feedback from mentors, coaches, or peers can be a game-changer, as they provide critical insights, share valuable experiences, and offer alternative viewpoints that help individuals navigate challenges with greater clarity.

The Mentoring Theory, proposed by **Kathy Kram (1985)**, highlights the importance of having a mentor to guide and support personal and professional development. Mentorship can take many forms—whether it's structured guidance in a professional setting or informal advice from trusted individuals. The key is that mentors provide not just solutions to immediate challenges, but also the wisdom to help mentees explore their own paths, encouraging self-reflection and growth. This support system becomes a backbone during periods of reinvention, enabling individuals to see beyond their own limitations and broaden their horizons.

Mentoring is a brain to pick, an ear to listen, and a push in the right direction.

-John Crosby, American Politician

A compelling example of mentoring in the tech industry is Marissa Mayer, former CEO of Yahoo. Before taking the helm at Yahoo, Mayer was one of Google's first employees and worked closely with Larry Page and Sergey Brin. Under their mentorship, Mayer developed a deep understanding of product design, user experience, and the intersection of technology and business. One particularly valuable piece of advice she received from Sergey Brin was to "always follow your curiosity." This principle guided her decision-making throughout her career and played a crucial role in her success at both Google and Yahoo. Mayer's journey illustrates how mentorship can not only shape leadership skills but also empower individuals to make bold career moves and drive significant organizational change.

Step 5. Seek Feedback and Mentorship: Leverage External Perspectives

Feedback and mentorship, however, are not about dictating decisions or providing a roadmap to follow blindly. As John C. Crosby puts it: "Mentoring is not about telling people what to do; it's about helping them discover what they want to do." This means that mentors serve as facilitators of self-discovery, offering the space and guidance to help individuals uncover their own aspirations, motivations, and goals. Through this process, those in the midst of reinvention can leverage their mentor's experiences and insights to make more informed, confident decisions. Mentoring is not about telling people what to do; it's about helping them discover what they want to do. By seeking feedback and mentorship, individuals can continuously refine their reinvention journey. The external perspective helps to challenge assumptions, refine strategies, and build the confidence needed to take risks and pursue bold new directions. Whether it's career advice, life transitions, or personal development, engaging with mentors brings in the experience and wisdom that accelerates growth, ensuring the journey is not walked alone but with the insight and support of others.

Step 6. Adapt and Iterate: Be Flexible and Responsive

Reinvention requires flexibility, adaptability, and a willingness to continuously iterate based on new insights and feedback. This idea is well captured in the Lean Startup Methodology by **Ries (2011),** which emphasizes the importance of learning from experiences, adjusting strategies, and refining approaches in real-time to stay aligned with evolving goals. Reinvention is not a linear journey; it's an iterative process that demands openness to change and a readiness to pivot when necessary.

Take the example of Ingvar Kamprad, the founder of IKEA, who continually adapted and iterated on his business model. Kamprad started IKEA as a small mail-order business selling various products. However, after encountering challenges related to the high costs of shipping bulky furniture, he revolutionized the concept by designing flat-pack furniture that could be easily assembled by customers. This adaptation not only reduced shipping costs but also allowed IKEA to offer affordable products to a global market. Kamprad's willingness to experiment, learn from setbacks, and iteratively improve his business approach transformed IKEA into one of the most successful global furniture brands.

The most successful people are those who are good at adapting to change

- Brian Tracy, Motivational Speaker

What makes Kamprad's story even more fascinating is that he never stopped evolving. Throughout IKEA's growth, Kamprad adapted to changing consumer preferences, embraced sustainable practices, and redefined the customer shopping experience through massive retail showrooms that allowed customers to envision how products would fit into their homes. Kamprad's mindset of flexibility and constant improvement is a perfect example of how the ability to adapt and iterate can drive long-term success and innovation.

Step 7. Celebrate Milestones and Reflect: Acknowledge Achievements

Recognizing and celebrating achievements can boost morale, reinforce positive behaviors, and serve as a reminder of how far you've come in your journey of reinvention.

Consider the example of Serena Williams, one of the greatest tennis players of all time. Throughout her career, Williams faced numerous challenges, including injuries, media scrutiny, and even life-threatening health issues. However, she consistently celebrated her milestones—whether it was winning her first Grand Slam or coming back to the court after giving birth. Williams' ability to reflect on her victories, both large and small, not only fueled her motivation but also allowed her to maintain a long and illustrious career.

Each celebration became a stepping stone to the next challenge, and her reflections on these achievements helped her stay focused on the bigger picture—her love for the sport and her desire to leave a lasting legacy.

Success is not the key to happiness. Happiness is the key to success. If you love what you are doing, you will be successful.

- Albert Schweitzer, Theologian and Physician

Williams' approach illustrates how celebrating milestones can fuel further success. By recognizing her progress, she was able to recharge, reflect, and remain inspired for future challenges. It's a reminder that acknowledging your accomplishments, no matter how small, is a vital part of reinvention.

Success, after all, is not just about reaching the final goal but about enjoying and learning from each step along the way. By celebrating each milestone, you reinforce the habits and mindsets that propel you forward, keeping the reinvention process both fulfilling and sustainable.

EXERCISES

1. Self-Reflection Journal: Dedicate 15-30 minutes to journal your thoughts on these questions:

- What areas of my life or career feel stagnant and in need of rejuvenation?
- Are there any skills or knowledge gaps holding me back from achieving my goals?
- What personal strengths and passions do I want to leverage in my next chapter? Write your reflections daily for one week and review your notes to identify patterns or recurring themes.

2. Skill Acquisition Plan: Make a list of three new skills that could be beneficial for your growth. For each skill:

- Research online courses, workshops, or mentorship opportunities.
- Set a timeline for when and how you will learn each skill.
- Track your progress weekly, and celebrate small milestones.

3. Role Exploration: Identify three roles or environments outside your current comfort zone. These could be new job opportunities, volunteer roles, or leadership positions.

- Describe what excites you about each role and what challenges you may face.
- Outline a strategy for how you would adapt and thrive in each new environment.

4. Fear and Resistance Analysis: Choose a specific fear or resistance you are experiencing regarding change. Answer the following:

- What is the worst possible outcome if this fear came true?
- How likely is this worst-case scenario to actually happen?
- What are three actionable steps you can take to reduce the impact of this fear?

5. Dismantle to Rebuild Exercise: Choose one area of your life where you feel you are stuck. Imagine dismantling the current structure:

- What beliefs or habits would you break down?
- How would you rebuild this area to better align with your values and aspirations? Write a detailed plan on how you will take steps to "dismantle and rebuild" with intention.

Chapter 7: Balancing Success and Personal Well Being: Avoiding Burnout

7.1. Understanding Burnout

Success is often portrayed as the ultimate reward for hard work, yet it comes with hidden dangers—burnout being one of the most insidious. Achieving great things can be exhilarating, but without balance, success can take a toll on emotional, physical, and mental well-being. In the relentless pursuit of goals, individuals may find themselves grappling with exhaustion, helplessness, and reduced performance. Burnout, as defined by Maslach's Burnout Inventory (MBI), highlights three dimensions: emotional exhaustion, depersonalization, and reduced personal accomplishment **Maslach & Jackson (1981).** Recognizing and managing burnout is essential to sustain long-term success and personal well-being.

Consider the story of Naomi Osaka, a world-class tennis player who faced an emotional collapse after rising to fame. Osaka, known for her powerful performance on the court, struggled with anxiety and stress from the pressures of being in the global spotlight. Despite her monumental success, including four Grand Slam titles, the relentless grind and media demands led to burnout. In 2021, she famously withdrew from the French Open to prioritize her mental health, sending shockwaves through the sports world. This decision showed that even at the pinnacle of success, self-care must take precedence over performance. Osaka's willingness to take a break—despite the expectations placed upon her—marked a shift in how athletes (and individuals in high-pressure environments) approach well-being.

Her journey exemplifies the twist that success doesn't always correlate with happiness or health. The higher one climbs, the more important it is to strike a balance. Like Osaka, many individuals feel pressure to constantly perform at their peak, but without adequate self-care, burnout becomes inevitable. Her decision sparked widespread discussions about mental health in competitive environments, revealing that true success isn't just about winning—it's about sustaining personal fulfillment and health along the way.

This is particularly relevant in today's fast-paced, "always-on" culture. Whether you're a CEO, athlete, or artist, the lesson remains: sustainable success is not a sprint; it's a marathon. It's critical to regularly assess personal limits, take breaks, and invest in mental well-being. Like Osaka, learning when to step back can sometimes be the most powerful move forward. Success and well-being aren't mutually exclusive, but they require thoughtful management. By recognizing the early signs of burnout and prioritizing self-care, individuals can ensure that they remain at their best—not just for a moment, but throughout their careers and lives. Balance is not the opposite of success; it is the secret to sustaining it.

7.2. Difference between Burnout and Complacency

While burnout and complacency can both negatively affect performance and well-being, they stem from opposite ends of the engagement spectrum and manifest in distinct ways. Understanding the difference between the two is crucial to addressing them effectively.

Burnout is a state of emotional, physical, and mental exhaustion caused by prolonged stress or overwork. People experiencing burnout often feel overwhelmed, depleted, and unable to keep up with constant demands. It results from working too much, under excessive pressure, without sufficient balance or recovery time. A typical example of burnout could be a pilot working on multiple long-haul flights with minimal rest between shifts. This intense workload, combined with sleep deprivation, could lead to fatigue, slower reactions, and difficulty concentrating—which can be dangerous in high-stakes environments like aviation, where alertness is crucial.

On the other hand, complacency arises from a sense of self-satisfaction or contentment that often blinds individuals to potential risks or challenges. Complacency occurs when a person becomes too comfortable with their achievements, leading to a decrease in effort or attentiveness. Instead of burnout's emotional exhaustion, complacency manifests as a lack of motivation to strive for improvement or growth. Using the pilot example again, a highly experienced pilot may become complacent, assuming they've "seen it all". This false sense of security could cause them to overlook critical procedures, take shortcuts, or dismiss checklists, underestimating the need for vigilance—ultimately increasing the risk of errors.

While burnout results from working too much, complacency comes from not working enough or failing to actively engage with tasks. Burnout pushes individuals to the point of physical and emotional collapse, while complacency leaves them stagnating, neglecting growth and improvement.

In both cases, the consequences can be detrimental. Burnout can lead to a sharp decline in performance, with a lack of energy and engagement, while complacency can breed carelessness and a false sense of confidence, which might lead to overlooked risks and missed opportunities.

7.3. Setting Boundaries

One of the most effective ways to prevent burnout is by setting clear boundaries between work and personal life. This involves creating distinct times for work and relaxation, and not allowing work to encroach on personal time.

Boundary Theory by **Ashforth, Kreiner, & Fugate (2000)** suggests that individuals create and maintain boundaries between different life domains to manage stress and achieve a work-life balance. Effective boundary-setting helps individuals protect their personal time and reduce the risk of burnout.

A notable example of setting boundaries to prevent burnout in the tech industry is Susan Wojcicki, the former CEO of YouTube and a key figure at Google. Throughout her career, Wojcicki has emphasized the significance of maintaining a healthy work-life balance, especially in the fast-paced environment of tech.

Wojcicki advocates for creating distinct boundaries between work and personal life. She has been known to implement policies that allow for flexible working hours and encourages her team members to take regular breaks and vacations. By promoting an environment where personal time is valued, she helps to mitigate the risk of burnout among her employees.

In her leadership role, Wojcicki has also been open about her own practices. For instance, she prioritizes family time and has been known to schedule personal commitments alongside her professional responsibilities. This approach not only helps her recharge but also sets a precedent for her team to follow. She believes that a well-rested and balanced workforce is more productive and innovative.

Wojcicki's philosophy aligns with Boundary Theory, which highlights the importance of delineating between various life domains to manage stress effectively. By fostering a culture that respects personal time, she exemplifies how tech leaders can combat burnout and maintain high performance in a demanding industry.

Her insights serve as a powerful reminder that success in tech doesn't have to come at the expense of personal well-being. As Wojcicki puts it, "It's important to have a balance, to be able to recharge, to be able to spend time with your family."

This holistic approach to work and life not only benefits individuals but also enhances overall organizational health, encouraging creativity and resilience in a competitive landscape.

7.4. Incorporating Self-Care Practices

Self-care is more than just a trendy buzzword; it's a vital strategy for maintaining personal well-being and navigating the complexities of modern life. It encompasses a wide array of activities and practices designed to enhance physical, emotional, and mental health. From regular exercise and nutritious eating to mindfulness practices such as meditation and yoga, self-care serves as the foundation for a balanced and fulfilling life.

The Dorothea Orem: Self-Care Theory by **Hartweg D. (1991)** underscores the crucial role of self-care in preserving health and preventing burnout. This theory posits that individuals must actively engage in self-care activities to manage stress effectively and maintain a healthy work-life balance. By prioritizing self-care, people not only nurture their bodies but also cultivate resilience against the pressures of everyday life.

Arianna Huffington, founder of The Huffington Post and author of *The Sleep Revolution*, exemplifies the transformative power of self-care. After experiencing her own bout with burnout—a moment of reckoning that left her physically and emotionally drained—Huffington emerged as a passionate advocate for prioritizing well-being. She emphasizes that sleep, often overlooked in our fast-paced society, is essential for productivity and creativity. Her journey has led her to champion practices that promote mindfulness, such as taking regular breaks, practicing gratitude, and engaging in activities that foster joy.

Huffington's insights resonate with many who struggle to find balance in their lives. She believes that self-care is not just a luxury but a necessity for sustainable success. By embracing sleep as a fundamental pillar of health and well-being, she challenges the prevailing culture that equates busyness with productivity. Her message is clear: when we prioritize self-care, we empower ourselves to perform at our best and contribute meaningfully to our work and relationships.

Self-care is not selfish. You cannot serve from an empty vessel.

-Eleanor Brownn, Inspirational writer

In a world that often glorifies hustle and relentless ambition, self-care emerges as a revolutionary act of self-preservation. It's a reminder that our well-being is integral to achieving our goals and that nurturing ourselves is the key to unlocking our full potential. As Huffington states,

"When we prioritize our well-being, we unleash our creativity and capability, allowing us to navigate challenges with clarity and purpose."

By fostering a culture of self-care, individuals can cultivate a more resilient mindset, paving the way for long-term success and fulfillment.

7.5. Prioritizing Mental Health

Mental health is as vital as physical health in the quest for long-term success and well-being, especially when it comes to preventing burnout. Recognizing this importance is crucial in our fast-paced world, where the pressures of daily life can easily become overwhelming. Prioritizing mental health involves seeking support when needed, practicing stress management techniques, and addressing psychological issues proactively.

The PERMA Model, created by psychologist Martin Seligman in 2011, provides a powerful lens through which individuals can improve their overall well-being. By focusing on Positive Emotion, Engagement, Relationships, Meaning, and Accomplishment, the model encourages a balanced approach to living a fulfilling life. When integrated into daily practices, PERMA can play a pivotal role in strengthening mental health and guarding against burnout.

Take the example of Indian cricketer Virat Kohli, known for his dedication to mental fitness alongside his physical training. Kohli has spoken openly about the importance of mental well-being, emphasizing practices that keep him focused and resilient. He's discussed how mindfulness and meditation have positively impacted his performance, especially in high-pressure situations. By prioritizing mental wellness and self-care, Kohli embodies the essence of engagement and accomplishment from the PERMA model. His openness about the mental challenges faced by athletes has helped break down stigmas associated with mental health in the sports community.

Similarly, Bollywood actress Deepika Padukone has been a strong advocate for mental health awareness in India. After her own struggles with depression, she launched The Live Love Laugh Foundation to help others navigate their mental health challenges. Deepika's story highlights the value of relationships and meaning, two crucial elements of the PERMA model. By using her platform to promote mental well-being and support others, she underscores the importance of seeking professional help and creating a supportive environment that fosters positivity and growth.

It's not the load that breaks you down, it's the way you carry it

- Lou Holtz, American football coach

Both Kohli and Padukone demonstrate that addressing mental health proactively is crucial for well-being. Their advocacy for mindfulness, therapy, and creating meaningful connections aligns with research that shows the benefits of these practices for emotional regulation and stress management **Kabat-Zinn (1990).** Their journeys inspire many to take mental well-being seriously and integrate practices that promote holistic health and fulfillment.

7.6. Embracing Flexibility and Adaptability

Flexibility and adaptability are vital attributes for managing success without compromising personal well-being, particularly in the ever-evolving landscape of today's global economy. An inspiring example from Africa is Njeri Rionge, a prominent Kenyan entrepreneur known for her remarkable ability to pivot and adapt in various industries, from telecommunications to digital marketing.

Rionge co-founded Grapevine Limited, one of Kenya's pioneering internet service providers, at a time when the internet was just beginning to gain traction in Africa. Her ability to foresee the potential of technology and its implications for business allowed her to create a successful enterprise. However, the landscape was not without its challenges. The rapid pace of technological advancement meant that staying relevant required constant adaptation. Rionge's success can be attributed to her openness to change and her willingness to embrace new ideas and technologies.

In the face of market shifts and emerging trends, Rionge did not hesitate to modify her business strategies. For instance, as digital marketing began to transform the way companies engaged with consumers, she quickly pivoted to focus on that sector, founding Njeri Rionge Digital, a firm dedicated to helping businesses enhance their online presence. This adaptability not only ensured her relevance in a competitive market but also demonstrated her ability to thrive amid uncertainty.

Rionge has also spoken extensively about the importance of maintaining a balance between personal well-being and professional ambition. She believes that self-care is critical for sustainable success. Her approach highlights the need for entrepreneurs to prioritize mental health, embrace flexibility, and take calculated risks, which aligns with Rogers' Adaptation Theory. This theory emphasizes that those who are adaptable and responsive to their environment can effectively manage stress and avoid burnout.

Moreover, Rionge's story emphasizes the value of mentorship and community support in navigating the challenges of entrepreneurship. She actively participates in mentorship programs, helping young entrepreneurs develop their skills and resilience. This focus on giving back reflects a commitment to fostering a supportive ecosystem for future leaders, ensuring that the cycle of adaptability and success continues.

The greatest glory in living lies not in never falling, but in rising every time we fall.

- Nelson Mandela,

President of South Africa [1994 A.D. to 1999 A.D.]

Balancing success with personal well-being is essential for avoiding burnout and achieving long-term fulfillment. By understanding burnout, setting boundaries, incorporating self-care practices, prioritizing mental health, and embracing flexibility, individuals can maintain their health and happiness while pursuing their goals. This holistic approach ensures that success is sustainable and enriching, without sacrificing personal well-being.

7.7. The Role of Mindfulness: Techniques for Staying Grounded and Focused

Mindfulness has emerged as a vital practice for enhancing well-being, especially in our fast-paced, high-stress environments. By cultivating mindfulness, individuals can experience profound improvements in their ability to manage stress, enhance focus, and achieve emotional stability. This chapter delves into the transformative power of mindfulness, offering practical techniques that can easily be woven into daily life.

At its core, mindfulness is about paying attention to the present moment without judgment. This practice encourages individuals to become fully aware of their thoughts, feelings, and surroundings, enabling them to respond thoughtfully rather than react impulsively.

Mindfulness isn't difficult, we just need to remember to do it.

— Sharon Salzberg, Author and teacher of Buddhist Meditation Practice

This quote serves as a reminder that the essence of mindfulness lies in its simplicity and accessibility.

One effective method for integrating mindfulness into daily life is through yoga. Yoga combines physical postures, breathing exercises, and meditation, creating a holistic approach to well-being. Not only does yoga enhance physical fitness, but it also promotes mental clarity and emotional resilience. By focusing on the breath and the body during practice, individuals learn to anchor themselves in the present moment, which can significantly reduce feelings of stress and anxiety.

Research supports the numerous benefits of yoga as a mindfulness practice. A study published in *Psychosomatic Medicine* found that individuals who practiced yoga regularly reported lower levels of stress and anxiety and improved overall mental health **Cramer et al., (2013).**

In addition to yoga, there are several other practical techniques individuals can use to cultivate mindfulness. For instance, mindful breathing exercises can be done anywhere, at any time. Simply taking a few moments to focus on your breath—inhale deeply through the nose, hold for a few seconds, and exhale slowly through the mouth—can help center your thoughts and alleviate stress.

Mindful walking is another technique that encourages individuals to engage fully with their environment. Instead of rushing from one place to another, walking mindfully involves paying attention to the sensations in your feet, the rhythm of your breath, and the sights and sounds around you. This practice not only grounds you in the moment but can also serve as a form of moving meditation.

Lastly, maintaining a gratitude journal can significantly enhance mindfulness by encouraging reflection on positive experiences. Taking time each day to jot down a few things you are grateful for shifts focus away from stressors, fostering a sense of contentment and well-being.

Incorporating mindfulness into daily life is not just about reducing stress; it is about enriching one's overall experience. As individuals become more mindful, they find themselves better equipped to handle challenges, enhance their focus, and cultivate a greater sense of fulfillment.

7.8. Maintaining Work Life Balance: Strategies for balancing ambition with a fulfilling personal life.

In today's fast-paced world, the relentless pursuit of success often leads individuals to compromise their personal well-being and relationships. However, maintaining a healthy work-life balance is crucial for long-term happiness and productivity. Let's explore strategies for balancing ambition with a fulfilling personal life, ensuring that success does not come at the expense of well-being.

Prioritizing What Matters Most

One of the fundamental strategies for achieving work-life balance is to clearly define your priorities. Understanding what truly matters—be it family, health, or personal growth—enables you to allocate your time and energy effectively. Indra Nooyi, the former CEO of PepsiCo, exemplifies this approach. She often spoke candidly about the challenges she faced in balancing her demanding career with her responsibilities as a mother. Nooyi emphasized the significance of being fully present in whatever role she occupied at any moment, whether as a CEO or a parent. The truth, she argues, lies in understanding your priorities and making conscious choices accordingly. This mindset allows individuals to manage their commitments without sacrificing their health or family relationships. Support from family, friends, and colleagues is vital in maintaining work-life balance. Indra Nooyi often acknowledged the role of her family and support network in her journey. Having people who understand your goals and challenges can provide encouragement and motivation during busy times.

In a study published in the *Harvard Business Review*, researchers found that employees with supportive relationships at work are more likely to be satisfied and engaged in their jobs. This reinforces the idea that prioritizing relationships is essential for both personal and professional success.

Setting Boundaries

Establishing clear boundaries between work and personal life is crucial for preventing burnout and maintaining relationships. This involves setting limits on work hours, being mindful of work-related stress, and making time for personal activities.

Boundary Theory suggests that individuals manage the boundaries between their work and personal lives through the processes of segmentation and integration. Effective boundary management can reduce work-life conflict and enhance overall well-being **Ashforth, Kreiner, & Fugate (2000).**

Tony Fernandes, the CEO of AirAsia, serves as a remarkable example of a leader who understands the importance of setting boundaries to maintain work-life balance. Under his leadership, AirAsia has grown into one of Asia's most successful low-cost airlines, but Fernandes has consistently emphasized that success should not come at the expense of personal well-being.

Fernandes has publicly shared his experiences with the high demands of running a large airline. He acknowledges the intense pressure that comes with the role but emphasizes the necessity of maintaining balance in life. He advocates for setting specific times for work and personal activities, ensuring he has time for family, fitness, and personal interests.

I always did something I was a little not ready to do. I think that's how you grow.

- Marissa Mayer, CEO of Yahoo Finance [2012 to 2017]

One of the notable practices Fernandes follows is his commitment to fitness and well-being. He often engages in activities like running and cycling, which not only keep him physically fit but also help clear his mind and manage stress. By prioritizing his health and fitness, he demonstrates how setting boundaries around work and personal time is critical for mental clarity and resilience. Research shows that employees who maintain clear boundaries report higher job satisfaction, lower stress levels, and improved mental health **Kossek et al., (2012).**

Fernandes has also been vocal about the importance of his family and personal life, making it a point to spend quality time with loved ones. He believes that leaders should encourage their teams to do the same, fostering a culture of respect for personal time. This approach not only enhances the overall morale within the organization but also promotes a healthier work-life balance for employees.

The most important career decision you'll make is who your life partner is. Stay with someone who will support your goals and boundaries.

- Sheryl Sandberg, American Technology Executive

For instance, when employees feel empowered to set boundaries, they are more likely to take time off when needed, engage in self-care activities, and return to work rejuvenated. Companies that prioritize employee well-being often experience lower turnover rates, increased productivity, and a more positive work environment.

Practicing Self-Care

Self-care is an essential component of maintaining work-life balance. Regular exercise, proper nutrition, adequate sleep, and mindfulness practices are vital for managing stress and sustaining energy levels. These elements not only enhance physical health but also support emotional resilience, allowing individuals to navigate the challenges of their professional and personal lives more effectively.

Research indicates that engaging in self-care practices can significantly improve mental health and overall well-being. For instance, regular physical activity is linked to reduced symptoms of anxiety and depression **Stathopoulou et al. (2006).** Similarly, proper nutrition and adequate sleep are crucial for cognitive function, emotional regulation, and stress management **Pandi-Perumal (2017).**

Michelle Obama, the former First Lady of the United States, serves as a powerful example of someone who has prioritized self-care amidst a demanding public life. During her time in the White House, she recognized the pressures of her role and the importance of maintaining her health and well-being.

Michelle Obama developed the *Let's Move!* initiative, focusing on the importance of physical activity and healthy eating for children and families. Through this program, she highlighted how regular exercise and proper nutrition can combat obesity and promote a healthier lifestyle for the next generation.

We think, mistakenly, that success is the result of the amount of time we put in at work, instead of the quality of time we put in.

- Arianna Huffington, Author

In her memoir, ***Becoming,*** Obama discusses how she learned to balance the rigorous demands of her position with the necessity of self-care. She emphasizes the importance of finding time for exercise, even when her schedule was packed. For example, she often rose early to work out, understanding that this commitment to her health allowed her to be more present and effective in her roles as a mother, wife, and public figure.

Moreover, Obama has openly spoken about the significance of mental health, advocating for awareness and open conversations about stress and well-being. She promotes the idea that self-care is not selfish but essential for maintaining the energy and focus needed to tackle life's challenges.

Time Management and Delegation

Effective time management is crucial for balancing professional ambitions with personal life. It requires a proactive approach that includes prioritizing tasks, delegating responsibilities, and learning to say "no" to non-essential commitments. This allows individuals to focus on what truly matters and aligns their efforts with long-term goals.

One of the most effective tools for managing time is the **Eisenhower Matrix**, developed by former U.S. President Dwight D. Eisenhower.

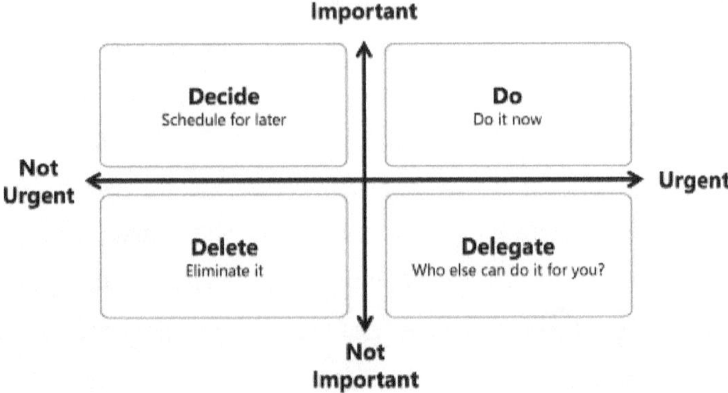

This matrix categorizes tasks into four quadrants based on their urgency and importance:

1. **Urgent and Important**: Tasks that require immediate attention and have significant consequences.
2. **Important but Not Urgent**: Tasks that contribute to long-term goals but do not require immediate action.
3. **Urgent but Not Important**: Tasks that may demand attention but do not significantly impact long-term objectives.
4. **Not Urgent and Not Important**: Tasks that are often distractions and should be minimized or eliminated.

By using this method, individuals can effectively prioritize their activities and ensure they focus on what contributes most to their long-term success. This systematic approach to time management can reduce stress and enhance productivity.

Satya Nadella, the CEO of Microsoft, exemplifies the importance of effective time management and delegation in his leadership approach. Upon taking the helm, he emphasized a cultural shift towards collaboration and empowerment within the company. Nadella believes that fostering a growth mindset not only enhances team performance but also allows him to manage his time more effectively.

Nadella is known for prioritizing key initiatives and encouraging his team to take ownership of their projects. This approach helps him balance his professional responsibilities with personal life, as he trusts his team to handle critical tasks and deliver results. In an interview, he noted, "I don't want to be the bottleneck in the system. I want to empower the team" (source: Business Insider).

You don't need to be a know-it-all; you need to be a learn-it-all.

- Satya Nadella, CEO of Microsoft

By delegating responsibilities and empowering employees, Nadella not only promotes a more efficient workflow but also creates a culture where innovation can thrive. This strategy allows him to focus on strategic decisions while maintaining a healthy work-life balance.

Success isn't about how much money you make, it's about the difference you make in people's lives.

- Michelle Obama, American Attorney

Balancing ambition with a fulfilling personal life requires intentional strategies that prioritize well-being, set boundaries, and foster flexibility. By practicing self-care, managing time effectively, and building a strong support network, individuals can pursue success without compromising their happiness and health. Remember, true success is not just about achievements but also about living a balanced, meaningful life.

EXERCISES

1. Self-Assessment: Understanding Burnout Triggers

- **Instructions**: Take 10 minutes to reflect and list the top five factors in your professional or personal life that contribute to feelings of burnout. Are these related to workload, lack of control, or unrealistic expectations?
- **Outcome**: Understanding what drives your stress allows you to address these issues with targeted solutions.

2. Defining Clear Boundaries

- **Exercise**: Write down three work-related and three personal boundaries that you struggle to maintain (e.g., not checking work emails after 8 PM or setting aside Sundays for family time). For each boundary, outline an action plan to enforce it.
- **Example**: "I will turn off work notifications on my phone by 8 PM and let colleagues know my 'unavailable' hours."
- **Reflection**: Discuss the potential benefits of these boundaries with a partner or in a group, if possible, to commit to maintaining them.

3. Daily Self-Care Routine Plan

- **Activity**: Create a daily self-care schedule that includes at least three practices. These can be as simple as taking a 10-minute walk, reading a book for pleasure, or engaging in a hobby.
- **Tip**: Set a reminder on your phone to engage in these activities. Regularly assess their impact on your well-being.

- **Tracking**: Keep a journal to note how these practices make you feel over a week and adjust your routine accordingly.

4. Mindfulness and Grounding Techniques

- **Exercise**: Practice a 5-minute mindfulness technique each day. This could include:
    - **Deep Breathing**: Inhale deeply for 4 seconds, hold for 4 seconds, and exhale for 4 seconds. Repeat this cycle 5 times.
    - **Body Scan Meditation**: Spend 5 minutes noticing how each part of your body feels, from head to toe.
- **Reflection**: Note any changes in your focus and stress levels before and after practicing mindfulness.

5. Work-Life Balance Vision Board

- **Activity**: Create a vision board that represents your ideal work-life balance. Include images, quotes, or symbols that inspire you to strive for balance.
- **Reflection**: Share your board with a trusted friend or mentor and discuss strategies to make this vision a reality.

6. Role-Play for Setting Boundaries

- **Exercise**: Pair up with someone and practice saying "no" in various scenarios (e.g., when asked to work overtime or take on additional tasks when overwhelmed). Take turns being the requester and the boundary-setter.

- **Objective**: Gain confidence in respectfully asserting your boundaries and learn from each role-play session.

7. Weekly Well-being Check-In

- **Exercise**: At the end of each week, schedule a 15-minute check-in with yourself. Ask:
    - What went well this week?
    - Did I honor my personal boundaries?
    - What will I do differently next week to improve my work-life balance?
- **Outcome**: Adjust your strategies as needed to maintain well-being and prevent burnout.

Your Best Performance is Yet to Come

The journey of overcoming complacency and striving for continuous reinvention reveals that true success is an evolving process, not a final destination. At every stage, it is crucial to remain vigilant, adaptive, and self-aware to avoid falling into comfort zones that hinder personal and professional growth. The key principles discussed, such as embracing failure as a learning opportunity, setting SMART goals, and fostering a culture of curiosity and perpetual learning, serve as cornerstones for lasting achievement and fulfillment.

Throughout this exploration, we've seen examples of influential figures who have successfully reinvented themselves by leveraging their strengths and remaining open to new experiences. The book emphasizes the importance of mentorship, self-assessment, and goal setting as essential tools for navigating change. By addressing signs of complacency early and adopting strategies for rejuvenation, individuals can maintain passion and purpose, ensuring their legacy is both impactful and enduring.

The message is clear: personal and professional reinvention is a deliberate and ongoing process. By cultivating resilience, staying grounded in purpose, and remaining proactive in self-improvement, anyone can craft a life defined not by past successes but by an unwavering commitment to future possibilities.

The belief that your best performance is behind you can be a trap that leads to complacency and self-doubt. But the truth is, **your best performance is yet to come**. Life is a continuous journey of growth, and every experience—whether it's a triumph or a setback—prepares you for an even greater achievement ahead.

When you rest on past successes, you risk halting your progress. **Don't rest on your laurels**, no matter how impressive your previous achievements may be.Instead, remind yourself that the skills, knowledge, and resilience you've gained so far are stepping stones to what lies ahead. Embrace challenges as opportunities to unlock new potential, push your boundaries, and discover untapped abilities.

Think of athletes, artists, or innovators who constantly strive to outdo their own records—not because their past wasn't impressive, but because they believe in the power of their future. You, too, have the capacity to evolve, to innovate, and to exceed your previous achievements. Stay curious, stay driven, and remember: the best version of yourself is not a memory but a goal yet to be realized. Keep striving, because your masterpiece is still in the making.

Regards,
Dr. Dhaval Maheta
Professor
Email: dhavalmaheta1977@gmail.com

References

Allen, T. D., Eby, L. T., & Lentz, E. (2006). The relationship between formal mentoring program characteristics and perceived program effectiveness. *Personnel Psychology, 59*(1), 125–153.

Arthur, M. B., & Kram, K. E. (1985). Mentoring at work: Developmental relationships in organizational life. *Administrative Science Quarterly, 30*(3), 454.

Ashforth, B. E., Kreiner, G. E., & Fugate, M. (2000). All in a day's work: Boundaries and micro role transitions. *The Academy of Management Review, 25*(3), 472.

Bandura, A. (1978). The self system in reciprocal determinism. *American Psychologist, 33*(4), 344–358.

Bass, B. M. (1996). *A new paradigm for leadership: An inquiry into transformational leadership.*

Biddle, B. (1986). Recent developments in role theory. *Annual Review of Sociology, 12*(1), 67–92.

Bisesi, M., & Kanter, R. M. (1984). The change masters: Innovations for productivity in the American Corporation. *The Academy of Management Review, 9*(4), 769.

Burton, H., & Dweck, C. (2020). Mindsets: Growing your brain.

Cramer, H., Lauche, R., Langhorst, J., & Dobos, G. (2013). Yoga for depression: A systematic review and meta-analysis. *Depression and Anxiety, 30*(11), 1068–1083.

Ericsson, K. A., Krampe, R. T., & Tesch-Römer, C. (1993). The role of deliberate practice in the acquisition of expert performance. *Psychological Review, 100*(3), 363–406.

Greenleaf, R. K. (2005). Greenleaf on servant-leadership: Who is the servant-leader? *International Journal of Servant-Leadership, 1*(1), 19.

Hartweg, D. (1991). *Dorothea Orem: Self-care deficit theory.*

Heifetz, R. A. (1994). *Leadership without easy answers.*

Kabat-Zinn, J., & Kabat-Zinn, M. (2021). Mindful parenting: Perspectives on the heart of the matter. *Mindfulness, 12*(2), 266–268.

Klamon, V. (2007). In the name of service: Exploring the social enterprise workplace experience through the lens of servant-leadership. *International Journal of Servant-Leadership, 3*(1), 109–138.

Knowles, M. (1977). Adult learning processes: Pedagogy and andragogy. *Religious Education, 72*(2), 202–211.

Kossek, E. E., Pichler, S., Bodner, T., & Hammer, L. B. (2011). Workplace social support and work–family conflict: A meta-analysis clarifying the influence of general and work–family-specific supervisor and organizational support. *Personnel Psychology, 64*(2), 289–313.

Kübler-Ross, E. (1973). *On death and dying.*

Lazarus, R. S., & Folkman, S. (1987). Transactional theory and research on emotions and coping. *European Journal of Personality, 1*(3), 141–169.

Leithwood, K., & Jantzi, D. (2000). The effects of transformational leadership on organizational conditions and student engagement with school. *Journal of Educational Administration, 38*(2), 112–129.

Lev Vygotsky's sociocultural theory of development. (2004). *An Introduction to Theories of Human Development,* 277–290.

Maslach, C., & Jackson, S. E. (1981). Maslach burnout inventory--es form. *PsycTESTS Dataset.*

Mezirow's transformative learning theory. (2023). *Encyclopedia of Sustainable Management,* 2365–2365.

Miliffe, K., Piccolo, R. F., & Judge, T. A. (2005). Consideration, initiating structure, and transformational leadership. *PsycEXTRA Dataset.*

Pandi-Perumal, S. R. (2018). Why we sleep: The new science of sleep and dreams by Matthew Walker, Ph.D. *Sleep and Vigilance, 2*(1), 93–94.

Rothwell, W. J. (2023). Succession planning. *Building an Organizational Coaching Culture,* 67–80.

Scott, J. C. (2009). The difference: How the power of diversity creates better groups, firms, schools and societies by Scott E. Page Princeton University press. 2007. 424 pages. $27.95 cloth. *Social Forces, 88*(1), 471–473.

Stathopoulou, G., Powers, M. B., Berry, A. C., Smits, J. A., & Otto, M. W. (2006). Exercise interventions for mental health: A quantitative and qualitative review. *Clinical Psychology: Science and Practice, 13*(2), 179–193.

Tierney, W. G., & Schein, E. H. (1986). Organizational culture and leadership. *The Academy of Management Review, 11*(3), 677.

Vallerand, R. J. (2015). Passion and emotions. *The Psychology of Passion,* 155–185.

Zagalo, N. (2012). Walter Isaacson (2011) Steve Jobs. *Comunicação e Sociedade, 22,* 211–214.

APPENDIX

SELF ASSESSMENT QUESTIONNAIRE

This self-assessment questionnaire is designed to help you reflect on whether complacency might be creeping into your life. By evaluating current habits, behaviors, and attitudes, one can gain insight to take proactive steps toward continuous growth and self-improvement. There are 50 statements given below. For each statement, rate yourself on a scale from 1 to 5, where 1 = Strongly Disagree, 2 = Disagree, 3 = Neutral, 4 = Agree, 5 = Strongly Agree.

Statement	Rating (1-5)
I find myself frequently setting new goals and aspirations.	
I often embrace new experiences that push my boundaries.	
I feel a sense of contentment with my current achievements.	
I reflect on my past accomplishments to inspire future actions.	
I actively seek opportunities to learn and grow my skills.	
My enthusiasm for my work and interests remains high.	
I appreciate diverse opinions, even when they challenge my views.	
I make an effort to identify and nurture emerging talent around me.	
I enjoy exploring new ideas and perspectives regularly.	

I welcome feedback as a tool for improvement.	
I adapt positively to changes in my environment.	
I maintain a balanced perspective about my capabilities and achievements.	
I strive to be disciplined and punctual in my commitments.	
I feel confident in my reputation while continuing to earn trust through actions.	
I regularly assess the effectiveness of my strategies and adjust accordingly.	
I prioritize maintaining important relationships and responsibilities.	
I actively seek motivation and purpose in my pursuits.	
I am open to adapting my personality and approach as needed.	
I take proactive steps to manage my time effectively.	
I engage in active listening rather than merely offering advice.	
I focus on long-term goals rather than seeking immediate gratification.	
I stay motivated despite the competitive landscape.	
I maintain healthy habits to manage stress and relaxation.	
I embrace challenges as opportunities rather than making excuses.	

I find joy in mentoring and supporting others' growth.	
I seek out constructive criticism to enhance my skills.	
I regularly attend workshops or seminars to expand my knowledge.	
I am excited to take on new responsibilities at work or in life.	
I enjoy collaborating with diverse teams to achieve common goals.	
I have a clear vision for where I want to be in the future.	
I actively reflect on my experiences to learn from them.	
I encourage others to share their ideas and perspectives.	
I remain curious about different fields or industries.	
I strive to create an inclusive environment for all voices.	
I take time for self-reflection to understand my motivations.	
I am willing to step outside my comfort zone to achieve growth.	
I prioritize personal and professional development in my plans.	
I recognize the importance of work-life balance in my life.	
I celebrate my achievements while looking forward to future goals.	

I continuously evaluate my strengths and areas for improvement.	
I seek out mentors to guide me in my journey.	
I maintain a proactive approach to problem-solving.	
I regularly assess my impact on others around me.	
I stay connected with industry trends and advancements.	
I value the importance of teamwork and collaboration.	
I embrace technology and innovations in my field.	
I find purpose in giving back to my community.	
I adapt my strategies based on lessons learned from failures.	
I feel empowered to make changes in my life when needed.	
I strive to maintain a positive mindset even during setbacks.	

Score Interpretation:

Add your scores from all 50 statements. The total will range from 50 to 250. As per your score interpretation is given below:

50–100: High Risk of Complacency — Individuals scoring in this range are showing signs of significant complacency. They may lack motivation, resist new challenges, and have become overly reliant on past achievements.

101–175: Moderate Risk of Complacency — This range indicates a balanced approach. While there is still a drive to improve, there are also signs of potential stagnation. Individuals here should be mindful of reinvigorating their goals and seeking new learning opportunities.

176–250: Low Risk of Complacency — A high score in this range reflects a strong sense of purpose, continual self-improvement, and active engagement with personal and professional growth.